The House Trap

The House Trap

By Alfred Gingold
Illustrated by Roy McKie

Workman Publishing, New York

"Everybody gotta be someplace."—Myron Cohen

Acknowledgments

Thanks to John and Pam Buskin, Randall Hatcher, Howard Leff, and Terrence and Sima Maitland for technical assistance and horror stories; to Michael Carlisle for his encouragement and support; to Sally Kovalchick and Peter Workman for making it all happen; to Lynn Strong for her invaluable help with the manuscript; to Charles W. Ross and associates for a job very well done; and to the Hang Chow Restaurant for providing luck and sustenance.

Library of Congress Cataloging-in-Publication Data

Gingold, Alfred.
  The house trap.

  1. House buying—Humor. 2. House selling—Humor.
3. Dwellings—Maintenance and repair—Humor. 4. American
wit and humor. I. Title.
PN6231.H73G56 1988   818'.5407   88-40227
ISBN 0-89480-615-7

Cover design by Charles Kreloff
Book design by Charles Kreloff with Stephen Hughes

Workman Publishing
708 Broadway
New York, New York 10003
Printed in the United States of America
First printing November 1988

10 9 8 7 6 5 4 3 2 1

For Helen

Contents

Part Two: Buying

Part Three: Making It Your Own

Appendices

Houseward Bound

Introduction

The closing is where hopes and dreams collide with reality, usually in some stuffy office. Here months of searching, days of negotiation and weeks of genuflecting at the bank are all supposed to pay off.

In front of you is an impressive amount of paper. These documents are called *instruments,* a strange thing to call documents until you realize that real estate people use strange terms for everything. For example:

◆ Real estate professionals say *dwelling.* Normal people say *house.*

◆ Real estate professionals say *half-bath.* Normal people say *extra toilet.*

◆ Real estate professionals say, "It's a very special kind of property." Normal people say, "This property is condemned."

◆ Real estate professionals say "last-minute closing costs and carrying charges." Normal people say "extortion."

Among the instruments are the deed, the letter of commitment, a letter from the title company (whatever that is), a certificate of inspection, a certificate of occupancy, a certificate of certification, and somebody's dry-cleaning ticket that got mixed up with the instruments. Laying out all these papers so you can look at them covers quite a large table, but not to worry: enough space has been left for your checkbook. Seated around you are more people than you'd expected (see "Who Are Those Guys, Anyway?" p. 95) and they all look preternaturally chipper, even if it's seven o'clock in the morning and raining. Why shouldn't they? You owe them all money.

The closing is when many home buyers first experience the headache, watery knees and sweaty confusion that are part of the total homeowning experience. And it's only the beginning. As a homeowner, you'll get used to paying strangers for reasons you understand only dimly.

Introduction

Every year, millions of Americans buy houses. This exhilarating experience leaves us anxious, depressed and in debt. And why not? Much is at stake. It is a great expense and a serious commitment. And more often than not, you're guided by ignorance,[1] misinformation,[2] guile[3] and self-deception.[4] Seldom do you know less about what you're getting than when you buy a house.

Think of this volume as comfort and companion through the horrors to come.

---

[1]. Yours.

[2]. Sellers, brokers and contractors all dispense this free of charge.

[3]. Everyone's.

[4]. Pride often cometh before a house. See "The Argument from Fantasy," p. 12.

Part One:
Searching

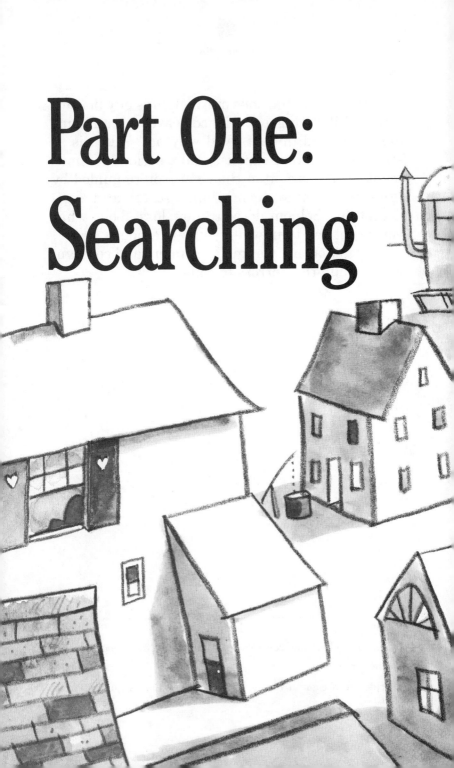

Home Is Where Your Stuff Is

---

*What's the matter with
where you are now?*

Before you go and do something extreme, like thumbing through Sunday's real estate section, think how happy you are in a place you don't own.

Perhaps you still live with your parents, where your cozy room and the perpetually stocked refrigerator almost make up for being too tall for your bed and too old for a curfew. Perhaps you serve in the armed forces: less cozy than your folks' place, no doubt, but they do serve big portions and provide valuable training such as folding hospital corners and learning to crawl face down through mud.[1] Or perhaps you're in prison, stamping license plates and hanging tough. Here the going may be a tad more stringent than at your parents', but at least you can complain to the guard about the leak in your ceiling.

If you're really lucky, though, you live in a nifty rented apartment, convenient to transportation, entertainment, dry cleaners and a decent Chinese restaurant.

Heaven on Earth: Your Rented Apartment

An apartment building is a miraculous thing. When I say miraculous, I mean it literally; no one knows how apartment buildings work.

For example, how does a toilet on the seventeenth floor of a high-rise flush without stirring a ripple in any of the sixteen toilets beneath it? And where does all the, uh, stuff go? It's magic. Even more amazing, toilets in an apartment building are frequently flushed simultaneously, especially during the morning rush and after the eleven o'clock news.

Try flushing all the toilets in a house. The water will swirl ominously, rising in each bowl slowly, slowly. Choking noises will issue from all

---

1. And, of course, there's no place like the army for stocking up on chinos.

the drains, even those in the kitchen and garage, and you'll probably have to call a plumber (one of those guys with wrenches). Two people cannot flush at the same time in a single-family dwelling.

Incinerators are another miracle of apartment living. You just take dainty bags of tasteful, apartment-style garbage (empty pantyhose eggs and Chinese food cartons, for the most part), open a little metal door and—whoosh!—there it goes.

For a homeowner, getting garbage out of the house is not so simple. It has to be sorted into categories (wet, dry, recyclable, nonbiodegradable, inert, ert, really smelly, no-so-bad, etc.). Then you have to leave it in carefully labeled plastic bags for some big guy to take away. In a better world, the super would take care of it.

But the grim truth is: houses do not have supers. Let *that* sink in for a moment.

Why do you think they call them supers?

As a Rule, Houses Do Not Have Supers

Superintendents are the key to domestic bliss, when you can find them. Plied with the correct blend of bribery, threats, and pleas for mercy, your super will eventually come to your apartment and fix a leak, turn off the radiator or hang a picture.

Nothing remotely like this happens in a house. Each of these tasks has to be done by separate home maintenance professionals. And you have to contact each of them, make an appointment, and wait around for them to show up (usually in about three weeks). Then you have to pay them. For the leak, you'll need a plumber (the one with wrenches). To turn off the radiator, things can get really complicated—especially if your home doesn't have one and you have to figure out how the place is heated. Hanging the picture can be really difficult, requiring consultation with your architect, decorator, local landmark committeewoman (if your house is old) and your spouse (even if it's not).[2]

Yes, a new home will challenge your health, your wealth and your sanity. So how could you even think of buying one?

---

2. You probably have a spouse, perhaps a burgeoning family. Why else would you be giving up your apartment?

Pathways to Real Estate

And How to Block Them

There are many cogent, sober arguments in favor of home ownership, and you may even believe them.

Silly, silly you.

Let's not be rash. Do you really, truly need a house, or do you only *think* you do? Innumerable hidden and not-so-hidden persuaders are conspiring to get you to a closing. Look before you leap.

The Argument from Fantasy

Imagining the home of one's dreams is a normal, even popular pursuit. No matter how comfortable they already are, some people like to waste their time musing about a fireplace in every room, an Olympic-size kitchen or their very own weathervane. My own dream house has a doorman.

Just don't confuse fantasy with something you're going to buy and live in. Dream houses do not need down payments or insurance. Dream houses do not require you to contemplate the difference between blown-in cellulose and foil-faced batt insulation. Dream houses have no mildew just to the left of the bathroom sink. Dream houses are the antithesis of real estate.[1]

"We Are the World" Complex

This is the intense desire to own a part of the earth, to put down roots as if you were a daffodil. "Land," you find yourself muttering, perhaps clutching a pebble as you dust around your potted cactus. "They ain't makin' any more of it. Upon this rock I will build my Cape Cod."

"Real property" consists of land and what's on it—usually a house. Anyone who's ever watched a

---

1. Later, when you're househunting, stay away from any house that has an herb patch outside the kitchen. The seller is gambling that there's an herb patch in your dream house and that you'll be so charmed you won't notice the bulge in the wall by the window (see "The Bulge Problem," p. 73). You can always put in your own damned herb patch.

rainstorm wash away his lawn knows that you can never own real property the way you own, say, your winter coat. Your winter coat just hangs there waiting for you. Stick a few mothballs in the pockets and you're fine. But real property does whatever it wants. Roof shingles loosen; pipes crack; the foundation settles.

Real property is a living, changing thing—like a goiter.

Your Expanding Family

It's human nature to want more room. It is to this basic desire that we owe both the exploration of outer space and the invention of the loft bed.

If you have children, chances are they've gotten bigger and noisier since you last looked. Soon every available nook and cranny will be filled with cheesy sneakers, rusting skates and heavy-metal albums. Eventually, you'll be crowded out of your own closet and your favorite chair will be the final resting place of an abandoned stamp collection. Before you look for someplace bigger, ask yourself this: What's the hurry?

Lack of room can be good for you. Just think of the pioneers, crossing the plains in those stuffy Conestoga wagons. Or the early immigrants, packed into poky tenements (today available as condominiums). *They*

A need for elbow room.

never complained (as far as I know). Growing up cramped builds character. Abraham Lincoln grew up in a log cabin, without a full-size freezer or a rec room. Look how well he turned out.

The Argument from Finance

Some people decide to look for a house after meeting with their accountant. Ordinarily, an accountant is someone you see once a year to be told you earn too little, spend too much and keep records that will put you in Leavenworth if you're ever audited. The minute your income increases even slightly, however, the skilled CPA strikes:

Real estate: the safest gamble in town.

CPA: (*Fingering your crumpled receipts*) Hm. You know, you could really use a mortgage.

YOU: I could? I haven't even paid off last month's Visa bill.

CPA: You're wasting all that money on rent.

YOU: I'm not wasting it. It's my *rent.*

CPA: Yes, but what do you get for it?

Searching

YOU: My place?

CPA: (*Pounding desk*) No equity!

Equity is one of these words you'll have to get used to, like *amortize* and *points* (see "Be Sure You Bring a Lot of Checks," p. 93). All you need to know about equity is that you can either borrow against it, in which case you slide even further into debt, or sell your property, hang on to the cash and move into your car.

CPA: Look, you don't own your apartment, so you're not getting any of the increase in the value of the property you're inhabiting. That's, that's... *throwing money away*!

YOU: When you eat out, do you consider the money thrown away?

CPA: When I eat out, it's deductible.

YOU: By the way, there's this terrific new Chinese place around the cor—

CPA: For what you're paying now, you can live better and make money at the same time.

YOU: (*Suddenly interested*) Huh?

CPA: Of course, your month-to-month expenses will be greater, especially after we factor in taxes, insurance and utilities, so you'll have to maintain your current level of income—more, of course, if you get an ARM and rates go up.

YOU: What's an—

CPA: The down payment will also present an obstacle. But what are savings for? Real estate is the best investment there is!

YOU: (*On the fence*) I don't know, the whole thing sounds sort of dangerous.

CPA: And I see signs that you can afford more than you think.

YOU: (*Hooked*) I can?

CPA: (*Fingers flying over calculator*) Let's see...

Your accountant comes up with a number that makes you gasp, arrived at by calculating your earnings during the most profitable ninety seconds of your life and assuming you'll make that much every ninety seconds till you're sixty-five. Since you want to believe this, you find yourself going along with his suggestions—and, soon after, deeply, deeply into hock.

It doesn't have to be that way.

Resisting Real Estate

With imagination and determination, you can postpone moving for years, maybe until the children have grown and it hardly seems worthwhile anymore. Below is a (very) personal selection of evasive tactics.

Consolidate belongings. Before you start ruining your weekends by spending them with brokers, go through your closet. Dispose of old or unused clothing and all the empty shoeboxes you've been saving. You'll see new possibilities right away. You may even decide to paint your closet and turn it into a den.

Clean your oven. This time-consuming process requires exhausting labor in an undignified position while inhaling noxious fumes. However, you now have a new enclosure in which to put your pots and pans. Watch your kitchen grow!

Buy a see-through plastic shower curtain for an open vista clear through to the other side of your bathtub, a cost-effective alternative to buying someplace with another bath.

Start a hobby, preferably something daunting like underwater photography or the tenor saxophone. Having such an interest will take your mind off your surroundings.

The last good real estate deal.

Act informed. Say things like: "I'm holding off till the market softens" or "Interest rates are *really* going to tumble." Refer to your neighborhood as "the region." Distribute checkmarks at random throughout the real estate ads and allow as how it's looking like it just might be time to think about starting to look. This technique requires that you never acknowledge the truth: the last good real estate deal in this country was the purchase of Manhattan for $24 in 1624.[2] Everyone since then has missed the boat.

Get sentimental. Every time someone mentions moving, look off into the distance and say dreamily: "Sure, it may be cramped, the fixtures may be old, the neighborhood disintegrating and the transportation inconvenient, but gee, you know, to me—it's home." Pat a wall fondly (but softly—you never know).

Not that any of these tricks will work for long. The homeowning bug is very hard to shake. Your moment of decision may come when a Pamper falls out of your attaché case. Or when a high-rise goes up next to you, impairing your hearing and blocking the view of your own fire escape. Whatever the reason, you will make a start.

In the days to come, you'll trudge through homes feeling as though your tax returns are stapled to your forehead. Prepare yourself.

---

2. The Louisiana Purchase was not a bad buy, either, but when you get right down to it, there's nothing like New York real estate.

Brokers, Agents, Realtors

Gypsies, Tramps, Thieves

Buying a house without a broker is possible, if you don't mind calling up strangers to ask if you can come look in their closets and flush their toilets. You need the services of a broker the way a man with a toothache needs a dentist: to inflict excruciating pain.

Sellers of real estate call themselves "professionals" to distinguish themselves from people who sell things smaller than houses, who are called "salesmen." *Brokers* are licensed to sell real estate by state authorities. *Agents* work under the supervision of a broker, just as the Artful Dodger worked under the supervision of Fagin. *Realtors* are brokers who belong to the National Association of Realtors and comply with its code of ethics (imagine what that must be like!). More important, realtors get to put a big "R" for "Realtor" on their business cards.[1]

It doesn't matter which kind of real estate pro you end up with as long as you use all three terms interchangeably. Brokers, agents and realtors hate it when you call them the wrong thing (see "Principles of Broker Harassment," p. 37). Anyway, finding the right broker for you is not a matter of credentials. It's a matter of scientific criteria: their names, their clothes, their gender.

What's in a Name?

Although most real estate offices are named after the brokers who run them, some are owned by huge conglomerates that could well be right-wing extremist organizations, like United Dwellings of America. Some brokerages have names like Country Bob's; the "folksy" approach usually means a messy office. Deep in the heart of Brooklyn,

---

1. Real estate pros are justly proud of their credentials and love to clutter their business cards with initials: C.R.S. (Certified Residential Specialist), G.R.I. (Graduate, Realtors Institute), A.R.W.B. (Association of Realtors Who Bowl). I, too, am proud of my professional qualifications and often follow my signature with the initials G.E.W.S.R.C. (Graduate, Evelyn Wood Speed Reading Course).

there's a place called Rustic Shores Realty; who are they kidding?

Choose a broker who calls you by your last name and return the favor. Be wary of men with hearty nicknames like "Woody" or "Jeep" or even just plain "Bill." Likewise, avoid women who go by coy diminutives like Steffi or Babs. The surname is best. Insist on it. Your broker is not your buddy.

She-Brokers

Buyer and seller alike feel the need for motherly concern during a real estate transaction. That's why so many brokers are such mothers. Some of them are also women.

The *Grim Divorcée* is a newcomer to the business, forced to find work when the mean son-of-a-

Your broker understands your needs.

bitch she was married to bribed the judge at the hearing and won a settlement that recently enabled him to splurge on new golf clubs. Grim Divorcées are formidable. When viewing houses with them, you see a lot of surprised homeowners jumping out of the shower or potatoed in front of the tube. The Grim Divorcée will have forgotten to call first and make an appointment.

She drives a car with a manual shift, "for better traction when scouting undeveloped land," she says heartily, but really just to intimidate you.

The *Stepford Realtor* is often a part-timer, but don't discount her expertise; she is strong, she is invincible, she is licensed. The Stepford Realtor is deeply, appallingly cheerful, always willing to blab about the weather or the traffic. She is the best informed of any realtor and actually knows things like the dimensions of the living room and whether or not the fireplace works. Once you give a Stepford Realtor your telephone number, expect three to eight phone calls a day. You'll live in fear of the day she makes good on her threat to invite you over for coffee. The Stepford Realtor wears tiny little earrings and a functional hairstyle, like Sandy Duncan's, that doesn't need a lot of fuss. She wears sensible shoes and drives a sensible car full of her kids' toys for you to sit on.

He-Brokers

The *Pillar of the Community* has been in the area a long time. Citations from the Knights of Pythias, the Elks, the Moose and the Klan cover the walls of his office, vying for space with thumb-tacked snaps of his family and sailboat; somewhere underneath it all is his dishonorable discharge, which some long-since-fired peon put up as a joke. The Pillar knows how to stir up business. At one of the innumerable church suppers he attends, he might tell a couple of *dear* old friends they need a change; before they know it, they're plonked onto some condominium development with drainage problems and their house has been sold to a young family, new to the area and unaware that the place is standing on reclaimed talc. The Pillar of the Community drives a big American car with a vanity plate bearing his first name or a clever abbreviation, such as "RLTY" or "BRKR." This is as close to wit as he has ever come, and he points it out to one and all. Out of the goodness of his heart, he will take care of any problems that might impede your closing, such as selling you the insurance you forgot about. He will sell you

A skilled broker can size you up with a glance.

more than you need and you'll pay top dollar for it, but at least you won't have to shop around. The Pillar of the Community has more than one way of getting at your money.

The *Good-Old-Boy-with-Sedan* comes from the area, like the Pillar, but from the other side of the tracks. He may have been a contractor (see "Good-Old-Boy-with-Truck," p. 120) before injury forced him to turn to white-collar crime. This background will make you think the G.O.B. knows what he's talking about when he tells you that everything in every house he shows you is just

fine. If you buy through a Good-Old-Boy, he'll
recommend a fuel company, a lawn service, a
plumber and many other local tradesmen. "Just
tell them you know me," he'll say, implying that
this will get you big discounts. Actually, the
tradesmen pay kickbacks to the Good-Old-Boy for
sending all his patsies their way and pass these
costs along to you. The Good-Old-Boy-with-Sedan
has been married several times,[2] and snapshots of
various children with various wives litter his
desk. The Good-Old-Boy practices other trades to
make his alimony payments. He may be a surveyor, lying to you about your acreage, or an
auctioneer, selling off old trash for a fat commission. Sometimes his sidelines are more exotic,
such as rewiring lamps or making stained-glass
flowers. He advertises these services on the sides
of his car, which are the only parts of the vehicle
he keeps clean.

Residential Display Tactics

Real estate professionals are appallingly well motivated.[3] In fact, once they get their teeth into your
neck, they just don't let go. Here are some of the
stratagems they use to get you to buy before you're
good and ready:

2. Divorce is rampant throughout all branches of the real estate
industry. After meeting a few people in the business, it's easy to
see why.

3. Unless you're trying to sell (see "Where Have All the Brokers
Gone?" p. 145).

◆ *"If you're interested, don't wait too long. I have two people who are interested already."* There are two people already interested in every house, condo, co-op and chicken coop for sale in the United States today. Ignore both of them.

◆ *Infirmities.* A surprising number of realtors seem to have limps or back problems. Mine wore an enormous back brace under his shirt, which he made sure to adjust every time he had to open (with much huffing) a garage door. These injured brokers are just faking so you'll feel bad about dragging them through yet another showing. You'll hurry through, skip the basement and be unable to come up with any questions at all. Before you know it, you'll have put in a bid out of pity.[4]

◆ *"My broker, my love."* Some brokers behave as if you're dating. The first appointment indicates interest; the second, an understanding; after the third, they start calling you "sweetheart" and "honey." Soon, you're supposed to go all the way and bid on something. If you don't, the broker will be hurt and cry, "I trusted you. How can you be so disloyal?" Don't respond; the broker will get over it.

◆ *"My broker, my friend."* This broker makes a great fuss of showing you only "things that are perfectly right for you." This means you have to go on and on about your taste in houses and clothes and movies; then the realtor shows you whatever's in the agency book. The idea that a broker will

---

4. I always bring a folding cane when I look at a property. Whatever problem the broker has, I'm in worse shape.

*"Now, here's
the closet,
I think."*

magically come up with a house that suits you
perfectly is a time-consuming fiction. When your
broker says "Tell me about yourself," just growl.

◆ *"Oh, THAT reform school!"* Selective blind-
ness is the most galling variant of the real estate
professional's basic gambit, the Out-and-Out Lie:

YOU:	The view over the backyard is lovely.
BROKER:	Yes, the landscaping is really a major feature.
YOU:	Say, what's that tower doing out there?
BROKER:	Tower? What tower?
YOU:	That huge tower with the searchlight on top of it.
BROKER:	(*Squinting*) Is that what that is?
YOU:	Yes, and those men—the ones in uniform.

Searching

BROKER:	Gardeners? Maybe it's a park. Of course, I'm no expert.[5]
YOU:	I've never seen gardeners with such big dogs.
BROKER:	(*Cornered*) Oh, *those* men in uniform. Why, that's a home, a sort of hostel really, for troubled youngsters.
YOU:	Troubled youngsters?
BROKER:	Teenagers, actually. But not to worry, they rarely make a break for it. And anyway, the fence is electrified.

◆ *Aggressive brokerage.* It's the nature of realtors to be pushy, but some of them overdo it. "Come on, I've shown you four houses already. Are you serious about buying or not?" is an assault that really doesn't bear answering, but it should tell you something. This broker could turn ugly in the face of direct questioning:

YOU:	Is the stuff wrapped around these pipes asbestos?
BROKER:	It was legal when they put it in. No one here has had a problem.
YOU:	I'm glad to hear that. I just want to know—
BROKER:	Are you bidding on the house or not?

---

5. Note agent's habitual shrug-off of responsibility for what agent has just said.

Househunters vary greatly in their methods of dealing with aggressive brokers. I myself favor skinning them alive and hanging them by their toes in the town square. Many state and local laws forbid, however.

◆ *Period charm.* Pillars in the living room, rotting floorboards in the hall: you're supposed to like them because they're *authentic.* I saw a house that had a stream of water bubbling through the basement. As my eyebrows reached my hairline, the broker said, "They built them this way back then. This way, you see, they always had a source of fresh water close by."

"In the *basement*?"

"What could be more convenient?" I think she said, but by then I was outside. Sometimes flight is the most eloquent response.

◆ *"It doesn't look like much, but all it needs is a few cosmetics."* Trust to your own instincts when your realtor says this to you. If the house looks recently bombed, if it appears that a cat has been fried in the fusebox, if there's a large hole in the bathroom ceiling, look on. *Cosmetics* is a term that brokers use to mean everything that happens to a house after the foundation is dug.

A problem with the wiring.

◆ *"To fix it up? Like new? Twenty thousand, tops. Of course, I'm no expert."* You have asked the price of renovating the entire house. Your broker, somehow mishearing you, has estimated the cost of a complete doorknob overhaul. To the broker, there is a fixed sum that nothing you will ever want to do to the house will exceed. It may be twenty thousand, it may be fifty, it may be three, but that is *it,* for anything: redoing the kitchen; landscaping the grounds; putting on a new roof; adding a porch; packing the whole place up and moving it to Belgium. Do not believe your broker's ballpark estimate for the cost of anything. He's no expert.

Gearing Up

Preparation for the Hunt

Shop for a home during the height of summer or the dead of winter. Your broker won't like it. After all, you'll have to drag around in stifling heat while the folks you drop in on enjoy cookouts on the patio. Or you'll skid up driveways and dump snow on the carpet. Sellers won't bargain much, either. Why should they? They know less chintzy people will be dropping by once the big spring or fall rush starts.

So why put yourself through such an ordeal? Simply for the sake of putting your broker through it *with you* (see "Correct Real Estate Attitude," p. 39). Watching a real estate professional bake or freeze makes your own discomfort worthwhile. Perhaps the broker will faint from the heat or slip on an icy pavement, while the owners wonder frantically if their insurance policy covers injuries sustained while trying to sell.

How Much Can You Spend for a House?

The rule of thumb for calculating your "range of affordability," as your broker will say, is that you can buy a house costing two to three times your annual salary.

Doesn't sound like much, does it?

Well, then here's another way. Tally your monthly expenses and subtract them from your monthly income, add 10 percent of your income over your income to cover insurance costs, fuel, necessary repairs, and miscellaneous miseries to which you have not yet been exposed. Throw in another 5 percent for boat rides, impulse jewelry and chocolate fits. The sum you're left with is what you can afford for mortgage payments. On a separate sheet of paper, compute what you can manage for a down payment, estimate what kind of mortgage you should have by consulting a mortgage guide, and that will give you the number you can afford.

Still depressing, no?

Interpretation of Real Estate Listings

Ad	Translation
Handyman Special	Requires bulldozer
Pond site	Bog with mosquitoes
Needs TLC	Don't buy unless you have assets of Shah
Charming	Tiny rooms, low ceilings
Cozy	Windows painted shut
Exciting neighborhood	Wild dogs and drug lords roaming free
Convenient to shopping, transportation	Abuts mall; 11 yards from Interstate
Income potential	If you don't mind sharing the bathroom
Enjoy country living	Refrigerators on porches

"I guess I pictured something different."

Keep a stiff upper lip anyway, even when your broker says it's impossible to buy a house with a flush toilet for the money you propose to spend. Remember that the National Association of Realtors forbids its members to show homes within a

Telltale Signs

Househunting can be a taxing business, no pun intended. Under the mounting pressure to make decisions that will affect your ability to afford hot lunches in the future, you'll begin to act strangely. Real estate professionals can smell your mood, so learn to recognize these danger signals:

Blind panic. In a blind panic you will not notice that the master bedroom has no electrical outlets and is much smaller than the master bathroom. You will arrive late at each showing, leave early and say nothing. There is no real cure for blind panic: *just calm down.* Slip off alone to a walk-in closet, slap yourself a few times and whisper, "Thanks, Sergeant, I needed that." No one will notice and it works! Or jog up the stairs en route to the second floor. The broker may be somewhat nonplussed, but pay no attention.

Nonchalance (false).[1] To conceal your desire to run away screaming, you may coolly fiddle with a drape, glance at a shelf, yawn and leave. Later you realize you don't remember a buyer's stated price range. The number you give is a challenge, a red flag to the realtor's bull. The price range of the homes you'll see will be 15 to 25 percent higher than what you say you can manage. Plan accordingly.

---

thing. Realtors see right through this one and realize it will mean extra showings. While it's always fun to irritate real estate professionals (see "Principles of Broker Harassment," p. 37), they might show you nothing but turkeys just for spite. False nonchalance evaporates like morning dew the minute you get interested in a place.

Misplaced sympathy. Real deals in real estate only happen because of someone else's hard luck: a job is lost, a marriage implodes, someone dies, and there's the house. It pays, therefore, to be on the *qui vive* for the misery of others while you're househunting. Knowing why a deal is a deal may dampen your zeal, but this is foolish. Enjoy. Remember, if everything were hunky-dory, the owners could hold out for a decent price and not have to sell fast and cheap to someone like you.

---

1. Not to be confused with nonchalance (real). There are individuals who househunt as a hobby, with no intention or need to buy. There are such people, just as there are people who like to cross-dress or eat dirt. Go figure.

Choosing Where to Live

You'll ponder many factors when selecting where to buy: tax base, housing stock, schools, police protection, number and quality of Chinese restaurants. Some househunters believe that reasonable considerations actually play a part in their final choice. Ha, ha, ha (see *"agony threshold,"* p. 42).

Before you move to a small town, attend a town meeting. There you'll find out what your

How to judge a neighborhood.

broker knows but won't tell you about garbage collection (the county dump is full), the zoning committee (about to turn your driveway into a service road for snow-plows) and the developer who wants to build a disco on the bird sanctuary.

Be wary when a realtor encourages you to look at a place because "you'll love where it is. It's a *new neighborhood.*" Avoid new developments with old WASP names like "Botsworth Square" and "West Patch Pocket." Those who have been displaced to make way for the gentrification may still be around, ominously wondering where all the wrought-iron streetlamps came from.

Self-Destructive Behavior

Looking for a house requires your full powers of loathing and mistrust. Some buyers believe they'll see better properties at better prices if they make

a favorable impression on their broker. These buyers appeal to their broker's expertise. Is there
enough light in the living room? (The broker
thinks there's plenty.) Is the bathroom tiling in
good condition? (The broker thinks it's fine.) The
impulse to befriend real estate professionals of
every stripe persists through all phases of home
ownership (see "Keeping Tabs," p. 134).

It is an impulse well worth resisting. Far better to go on the attack.

Principles of Broker Harassment

For the real estate pro, as for any salesperson, the
pitch is more important than the product. Raised
ranch, center hall colonial, Cape Cod—who cares,
as long as you buy one? For you, on the other hand,
the *house* is the important thing and the pitch is a
windy annoyance you put up with because the
broker has the keys. Keeping your broker confused
and on edge is the best way to get a little peace
and quiet in which to examine the offering. Here
are a few sure-fire techniques:

◆ Get your broker's name wrong. If he's Mr.
Foster, call him Mr. Grant. If her name is Anne,
call her Angela. Apologize fatuously and correct
yourself; then get it wrong ten minutes later, and
so on, right up to the closing.
◆ Break the flow of the broker's spiel with
irrelevant questions, misplaced observations or
out-and-out non sequiturs:

BROKER:	Now, it isn't very often that you see new construction with this quality of workmanship. Look at the way these kitchen cabinets operate. You can open them (*opens them*) or close them (*closes them*), whichever you choose.
YOU:	Hey, look! These people collect bisque figurines.
BROKER:	Sorry?
YOU:	I'm out here in the living room. Hey, you think we can work these little guys in with the house?
BROKER:	Well, I suppose we could find out, but I'm no expert. Let me just show you the sink. It comes with faucets.
YOU:	Wow—a jigsaw puzzle. I *love* jigsaw puzzles! How 'bout you? Listen, you look a little tired. I get tired around this time of day, too.
BROKER:	No, I'm fine, let's—
YOU:	I have a great idea! Why don't you just sit down and take a load off while I peek upstairs? I'll shout if I have any questions.
BROKER:	Maybe I will.

◆ If your broker points out a flaw, glom on to it and never let it be forgotten. Refer to "the house with that finished basement that isn't really finished" or "the fixer-upper—the one that needs a screen door."

◆ Your broker may try to draw you out so you'll waltz through houses, chatting brightly, oblivious to structural problems right under your nose. Maintain your mystery. Walk through a house in utter silence. Grunt. Nod. Make an occasional note on the grubby pad that you keep in your pocket. It takes grit to pull this off, especially the business with the pad. The effect is salutary, though. Broker and seller alike are unnerved by quiet househunters.

Don't be afraid to point out problems.

Conclusion: Correct Real Estate Attitude

In the course of buying and owning a home, you'll require the services of numerous highly trained individuals: brokers and agents, of course, as well as loan officers, appraisers, surveyors, title insurers, lawyers, contractors, roofers, masons, plumbers and many, many more. If you're lucky, they'll be late, slow, rude and expensive. If you're not, they'll be dishonest and incompetent, too. You'll pay anyway just to get them out of your sight. What else can you do? It's the way of the world.

The only weapon available to normal people at the mercy of the real estate industry is the power of *poor sportsmanship.*

When your broker raves about the view, poke suspiciously at the window frame with your pocket knife. "Checking for rot," you explain when the owner blanches (see "If You'd Only Known," p. 61). Whine in protest when your lawyer blames you for not bugging the bank enough. You don't buy and sell houses every day, like these clowns. Naturally you're on edge. Lighten the psychic load by venting a little spleen at every real estate pro you meet.

Offers and Counteroffers

You Better Shop Around

No one bids on the first or second house they see, blithely assuming there must be something better out there. All real estate professionals know this, so, like butchers pounding veal with the side of a cleaver, they break down your fibers by dragging you through the agency's backlist of unsold, unsound, overpriced hovels. Make the best of these useless forays by taking notes so you can tweak the broker with nitpicking questions about dumps you've seen weeks earlier.

Considerations such as price, location and whether or not there are enough bedrooms have no effect on your choice of home. No, as the days turn into months of futile, bumbling house calls, these concerns pale as you near your *agony threshold,* when the prospect of looking for one single second longer causes *delusions of habitability* in every house you see.

Just when you're about to give up in disgust for the season, a house will come along that you think is almost all right, sort of. The feeling of possibility grows within you overnight like a stomach virus. Perhaps you're onto something. What should you do?

List pros and cons about the house. Visualize yourself pulling into the driveway, flipping through the mail, pouring yourself a drink and sitting down with the evening paper. Then knock off for the day. Pour yourself a drink and have a look at the paper.

When you're able to think about the house for fifteen minutes at a clip without hyperventilating, proceed to the next step in your decision-making process: asking everyone you know what they think you should do.

What Are Friends For?

Call and tell them about it. Describe the rooms, the lot, the neighborhood. Ask if they know anyone from around there. Ask if, on the basis of what you've told them, they would move there. Ask if they'll come to visit.[1]

After your best friends, several acquaintances and whatever family members you still speak to have weighed in with opinions and you still feel the house is a maybe, arrange with your broker for further visits. Keep in mind, however, that once you've looked at a house three times, your broker will begin sleeping in your driveway.

Encounters with Owners

"Don't let us disturb you."

You will probably meet the owners on one of your visits. As all of you stand around feeling awkward, watch carefully for non-verbal communication among homeowning family members. Did Daughter blush when Dad said the tap water was fit to drink? The owners may offer coffee or a soda, but watch out if you're offered alcoholic beverages. They could be trying to blunt your powers of observation and resolve. Beer, wine and sherry, of course, do not count as alcoholic beverages.

Be as charming as you can when you meet the owners. Remember, your goal is to make them

---

1. Don't call the same friends too often about the same house. Let them rest and consolidate their views before approaching them again. Friends should be rotated, like crops.

divulge the worst secrets of the house and then let you have it for a fraction of what it's worth just because they like you so much. Failing this, you want to undermine their confidence in the value of their home. Do this by pointing out obscure problems in the form of compliments.

Example: "I love the way you've handled the space in the living room. It makes the room look so much bigger than it really is."

Caveat: Never suggest that anything is wrong with the taste of the owners, even if there are acrylic fur seat covers on all the toilets and a portrait of Elvis over the hearth with eyes that follow you around the room.

Making Your Bid

Do not insult the seller with a figure so low that he'll threaten to pound you into the ground like a tent peg. You want him to feel that your offer is a serious one, that you're a qualified buyer, that there will be no monkey business once you've gone to contract and, most important, that if your offer is not accepted, *there will never be another offer again. Ever.*

A bid should not be a clearly discernible percentage less than the asking price. Do not, for example, simply deduct 10 percent just because your broker tells you it's customary. The owners will know you're following the broker's advice and are, therefore, in his grasp (see "Whose Broker Is It, Anyway?" p. 46). No, a bid must be a *peculiar* number, one that will make both seller and broker expect that you *know* something about the property.

Use the following formula to calculate your offer:

Price = .20 (price) ± (100 × no. of yrs.)

In other words, subtract 20 percent of the asking price, then add or subtract your age times one hundred, depending on how nervy you're feeling when you talk to the broker.

Example: A house costs $200,000 and you are forty-three years old. Your offer then would be $174,300 or $155,700. Either figure is certainly low enough to cause the seller a sudden intake of breath, yet both seem too finely calibrated to be shots in the dark. Hours after your offer is received, the seller will be sitting around wondering, "Why one fifty-five *seven*? Why not one fifty-five *five*? Did they figure out that the dry mold in the dining room doesn't go away?"

Know Thyself

Schedule a complete physical exam before making your bid. Have your eyes checked, too. You may be in no condition to negotiate the purchase of a house. You may need a few weeks at Club Med to wind down before starting in later, when the market's loosened up. At the very least, go out for some Chinese food before deciding what to offer.

Whose Broker Is It, Anyway?

Brokers refer to home buyers as "customers," but the sellers pay their commissions so it's the sellers they serve. Never tell a broker what you're willing to spend on a house, since the sellers will know as soon as the broker can get to a phone.

Nor should you be intimidated by the broker's attempts to make you feel chintzy. These begin as soon as you make your offer and the broker's nose wrinkles as if you've just done something unspeakable in the elevator. The broker then says something like:

◆ "You're kidding, of course. Please tell me you're kidding."

◆ "Well, I think the owners will certainly be *surprised.*"

◆ "I don't think I can go to them with that offer. I have my health to think about."

Point out that federal law requires licensed real estate professionals to communicate all good-faith offers for properties shown by them regardless of whether or not they're satisfied with their cut. Who knows? Something like that may very well be true. Tell your broker that you're perfectly capable of picking up the phone, calling the owners and presenting an offer yourself. Point out that, although you're no expert, your offer could probably be a bit lower because the sellers would not have to pay a commission.[2]

---

2. I don't actually know anyone who's had the nerve to do this, but I'd certainly love to try (if I could manage it without stuttering).

Emotional Transparency of Real Estate Professionals

The house you're hoping to buy holds who-knows-what horrors, but brokers hold no such secrets. They reveal their intentions and feelings with utmost precision by declaring what they are not. If your broker says, "I don't want to rush you," he's trying to rush you. If, on the other hand, she says, "Don't worry!" you know she's worried and you are therefore doing something right. In any other business, such persistent denial would be considered pathological dishonesty; in the real estate profession, it amounts to integrity.

Getting into a Binder

Make your offer official by signing a written statement of the price and terms according to which you're willing to buy the property in question. This *binder* is accompanied by some refundable *earnest money*, perhaps a percentage of the purchase price or $500—enough to show that you know the importance of being earnest.[3]

Ornament the binder with as many *contingency clauses* as you can think of. Make your offer subject to: adequate financing, written permission from spouse, the

To bid or not to bid.

---

3. In monied communities, fingers or gold teeth may be required.

swallows' prompt return to Capistrano, structural report, termite inspection, seller's agreement to avoid stepping on sidewalk cracks until after closing, and statement of approval from your most tasteful friend. Your binder should also be subject to cancellation due to anxiety attack, but make sure the closing date can be extended thirty days if necessary to get your financing or head together. Contingency clauses are also called *jump-out clauses* because they can keep you from jumping out the window.

Twisting Your Arm

It's only because your broker is tirelessly fighting for you that the sellers are even considering your paltry offer—at least that's what the broker says, on the basis of which you can safely conclude that the broker is lying (see above). Stay cool during negotiations. Act as if you don't really want the house that much. Communicate only by telephone so your broker can't see the pulsing veins in your forehead. Whistle a happy tune during lulls in the conversation to show that you can. (Through the receiver, a tape recording sounds just as good as the real thing.)

There are as many ways to goose a buyer's offer as there are real estate professionals. Below are four standard counteroffer prods.

Gestalt brokerage. "I'm okay. You're okay. Let's talk reality. I think if there's no movement on your part—I mean in terms of, you know, like money—then that's it! I don't want to upset you."

Home-style. "Gosh, I'd hate to see you lose the house of your dreams over a few thousand dollars. It's really *you*—and so many closets!"

Snobberage. "I'm afraid you have to spend a bit more to purchase a dwelling in our community. Of course, I'm no expert."

Bleeding heart. "It's not the money, really, it's the *gesture*. They want you to have their house, I know they do. Another two or eight thousand and it's yours."

Choke Point

One day you will make an offer that's a lot more than you set as your limit. To convince yourself that you're driving a hard bargain instead of capitulating completely, you might demand that some old lawn furniture stay with the house or insist on specifying the date of the closing. Your broker will immediately agree to both conditions. After all, the furniture is probably rusty and, no matter what's in the contract, any broker knows that the closing date is determined by when the lawyers return from salmon fishing in Scotland.

Why are you doing this?

You make this offer because you have realized you cannot do without the house. It is all you have ever wanted, more than you ever will want. You must have this house even if it means paying too much for it. Your agony threshold has been reached. You've become delirious, as every house-hunter does before making the final offer. You have reached Choke Point.

Meanwhile, you rearrange the furniture where you are now. The space really opens up! Mortgage rates rise. The market softens. It's foolish to get trapped into a deal made in the heat of a seller's market now that it seems the recession has finally arrived. What's your hurry? Maybe you'd better go out for some Chinese and rethink the whole thing.

It is at this moment that the broker calls to say the owners have accepted your bid.

Open the bottle of champagne you've been saving; you'll be in no mood for a discretionary purchase now. Drink hearty! Just think of what you've done!

A drink on the house.

What Have You Done?

Although it's probably the biggest transaction of your life, your home purchase is undertaken with less knowledge and information than you would bring to ordering lunch.

In fact, the more enthusiastic you became about the house, the less clearly you could think or see when you were in it. Instead, you busied yourself during successive visits by tapping walls, twiddling the bathtub taps and staring gravely into closets, wondering what to say, and finally congratulating the owners on their abundant wooden hangers.

Fortunately, it's time for the inspection.

Part Two:
Buying

An Inspector Calls

Checking It Out

anks usually require a report from a house inspector or structural engineer before they'll give you a mortgage. This report gives you the pleasant feeling that a licensed professional has pronounced you safe from disaster. In fact, all an inspection means is that if there *are* major structural problems in your home, the particular licensed professional you hired didn't find them and is therefore not to blame for your rampant idiocy. In a word, tough.

Choose Your Inspector Wisely

This is difficult to do, because none of the advice you'll receive is trustworthy:

◆ The owners will tell you that their house was inspected last month and you can look at the report. Sure. They *like* to have their house inspected every so often just for the hell of it, just to make certain everything's up to snuff.

◆ Your realtor will tell you that Andy over on Dumpster Road does all the inspections in the area. ("He's not really what you'd call a licensed inspector, but he's a darn good contractor.") Andy will be over in a flash to tell you that the house is jimbob-okay and he'll throw in a free estimate on the work you'll need to make it really shipshape.[1]

What Kind of Inspection Do You Want?

An expensive one.

My home inspection cost $35 and was worth even less. Bargain-rate inspectors whip through a house before you can get out of your car, then say that everything looks pretty good but you just can't be sure. A first-rate inspector takes several hours and costs you several hundred dollars, but

---

1. Andy and your realtor are in cahoots. Andy gives every house a clean bill of health. The broker gets the sale, Andy gets the fee and, with any luck, a job, which will consist largely of further concealing the major structural problems he ignored in his inspection.

what you end up with is much more substantial: a comprehensive report concluding that all operating systems and structural elements of the house look pretty good but you just can't be sure.

Inspectors can never be sure, because there are limits to how closely they can inspect. In general, they're not allowed to lift up carpeting, puncture walls or move furniture. In some states, house inspectors are forbidden to bring their eyes into focus during working hours. These rules protect property and give a fighting chance to sellers with something to hide.

Hire an inspector who is familiar with the area and its housing stock. Ask for references and an explanation of why the fee is so large. Insist that you're prepared to bargain; a reputable inspector will refrain from laughing directly in your face. As a final assurance, find out if your inspector belongs to the American Society of Home Inspectors, an outfit devoted to three principles:

◆ Providing the home buyer with prompt, courteous residential examination services.

◆ Performing these services in time to beat the rush hour home.

◆ Wearing blazers adorned with the society's crest—even in bed.

Inspection Bewilderment

Failure to attend the inspection sends an immediate signal to seller and broker alike that they can have their way with you, and might even encourage the inspector to cut some corners.

You will understand little of what the inspector is doing, even if you're as experienced an all-around Mr. Fix-It as myself—and I count among my accomplishments painting a bookcase once. The average home is far more complicated than anything a normal person is used to dealing with. If the house is old, it was probably built by honest workmen who knew what they were doing and took pride in their labor, which is more than can be said for the generations of owners who've lived there since. New construction has the advantage of up-to-date technology and materials, but it has probably been assembled by butter-fingered wage slaves in the employ of sleazy developers who don't care if their lousy buildings fall down twenty minutes after title closes.

All the same you must be there, peering over the inspector's shoulder and asking questions at appropriate intervals to show that you're concentrating. To heighten the drama, consider wearing a surgical mask and goggles. You may ruffle the owners, especially if you frighten the children, but you can justify yourself by claiming you want "protection against fumes—just to be on the safe side." In addition, carry in plain sight a pocket watch, a small rubber ball and a flashlight. The inspection will be finished before you can use them (see "If You'd Only Known," p. 61), but their presence makes you look formidable.

Write down your questions in advance so you don't forget them. They should suggest a keen knowledge of residential construction, not your need to be reassured.

Good question: Is the flashing around the ventilation slots secure?

Bad question: Do you think there's enough kitchen storage?

The Fine Print

Before you know it, the inspection is history. The house is pronounced "nice and solid" except for "a few little problems" (see "Rude Awakenings," p. 107) that your broker maintains can be "addressed at the closing," fully aware that by then you won't be able to remember your name. The broker will start bugging you to call your lawyer, get your mortgage, sign the contract. The ball really starts to roll.

One night you pick up your inspection report and leaf through it. There you see a lengthy series of disclaimers stating clearly that the inspection in no way guarantees or warrants the condition of the house. Should your house turn out to be in much worse shape than the inspector told you, the report states, don't bother us.[2] Like other real estate professionals, your qualified house inspector is no expert. In a word, tough.

Too late now. How could you have prevented this situation?

---

2. Some inspection companies offer insurance, paying anything up to a very tiny maximum over an enormous deductible should any problems arise within a year after the inspection, assuming of course that you can get them on the phone.

If You'd Only Known

How to Look at a House

Most normal people wouldn't recognize a major structural problem if it bit them on the nose. Such defects are not difficult to conceal, especially by people who will stop at nothing to do so. While you won't be able to determine everything that can go wrong with a house once you buy it, you can, with a little preparation, avoid an utter turkey.

Ground Zero: The Foundation

Begin your tour of the house by checking its *foundation,* which is usually in the basement (but not always—see p. 63). A foundation is a hole in the ground with walls. Examine the walls for vertical cracks. The meaning of these cracks depends on when you find them:

◆ Before you buy, they are a good sign because, as your broker will tell you, they show that the house has "settled into its foundation."

◆ After you've bought, they are a terrible sign because, as your contractor will tell you, they indicate dangerous shifts in the earth's crust that threaten property values throughout your zip code.

While you're downstairs, examine the walls for peeling paint or damp spots. These indicate *moisture,* which is how brokers refer to water. At the same time, take a look at any hunks of wood in the basement that look as if they're holding up the house. These are called *sills, joists* and *beams,*[1] and should appear solid and firm. Pick at one with your pocket knife. If the wood is soft and porous, it is *rotten*; this condition may be caused by water (see p. 72) or insects (p. 110). Do not stick around to find out which. If the wood is solid, the house may still have a rot problem, but one that has not yet progressed to where your pocket knife is.

---

1. There is no need to learn these confusing terms. Just remember the phrase *structural members,* so you don't have to say "those hunks of wood that look as if they're holding up the house."

Use your flashlight in the basement even if it is well lit. Always assume there is something important for you to see in some dark, out-of-the-way corner. Besides, you'll look foolish to your broker if the only use you have for your flashlight is examining dustballs under the bed.

On the first floor, check again to see that the floors are level. It's bad enough to buy a sinking house, without buying one that is sinking at a rakish angle. You'd be seasick all the time. Test for levelness by placing a rubber ball in the middle of each room. If it rolls to one side, leave. If it stays put, you can safely assume the joists are meeting the sill at the proper angle and the house is right

---

Houses Without Basements

Some houses lack basements because the ground underneath is too wet or the builder is too cheap. Basementless homes are popular in Florida, where the water table can rise to your ankles,[2] and in Texas, where presumably no one needs the storage. A *crawlspace* is an unsatisfactory basement substitute that requires a contortionist's skills to reach. Eventually it will become your children's favorite hiding place because you can't get at them without scuttling into the crawlspace on your knees, like a Toulouse-Lautrec impersonator.

---

2. The state of Florida presents many unusual homeowning challenges. See "Waterbugs," p. 110, and "Reptiles," p. 111.

as rain. On the other hand, you might simply have placed the ball on a shag carpet. Be observant!

Diddler on the Roof

The roof is the advance guard of the house. It engages the elements first and provides the most fundamental protection from them. As such it is always a source of anxiety and concern. If it's old, you wonder when you'll have to replace it. If it's new, you wonder when you'll have to repair it.

Every roof needs adequate *runoff.* You can't just let the water that is ready to fall off your roof go straight over the sides. First of all, the random dripping would keep you up and drive you crazy. Then all the water would end up in your basement. To ensure proper runoff, all roofs must have *gutters* that drain the water to *leaders.*[3]

Check the southern exposure of the roof. This side gets the worst beating from the sun's rays because of the rising and setting of the sun in the south. (Well, actually it rises in the east and sets in the west, but you'd never know it to look at the southern exposure of your roof.) Asking about it will add ineluctably to your mystique.

Trying to decide which way is south will probably keep you too preoccupied to ask what the roof is made of and whether or not it keeps the weather out (should you buy, you'll find out when it rains). The most common roofing materials are:

---

3. Saying "Take me to your leaders!" as the inspector gets ready to climb up on the roof is a fine way to offset the *gravitas* that prevails during the inspection, especially if the inspector's afraid of heights.

Material	Description
Slate	Unbelievably expensive; breaks easily; requires specially trained, dying breed of craftsfolk to repair or replace
Asphalt shingle	Smells funny when wet; cracks in cold; retains heat in summer
Wood	Leaks; smells; rots
Metal	Bends; rusts; corrodes

If price is no object, you might consider a thatched roof, certainly the cutest roof of all, especially if

Geographical Note

The ability to talk about the "west wall" of a dwelling instead of "the wall with the cracked window in it" is a badge of savvy you can't do without in the cut and thrust of househunting. Here are the differences between the various directions: East is East and West is West and ne'er the twain shall meet. The East is red. Go West, young man. True and tender is the North. The South shall rise again.

That's it. They call the wind, of course, Maria.

you don't mind living under a fire hazard teeming with mice and spiders. From a distance, a house with a thatched roof looks like Don King.

A Tale of Two Sidings

Siding is what's on the sides of the house. There are two types of siding: Real and Fake. Real Siding is made of wood, brick or stones.[4] There aren't many stone houses around anymore; they are comfortable only for short people, as their ceilings are so low you wonder how the Pilgrims managed with those pointy hats. Brick houses usually look like banks. Wood siding comes in many varieties, from vertical tongue-in-groove cedar (Contempo-Grotesque) to Novelty Siding (not as much fun as it sounds) to Good Old Clapboard.

Fake Siding is made of aluminum or vinyl and has an embossed wood grain that fools no one. While Real Siding must be painted every few years, Fake Siding can be cleaned with your garden hose.

Fake Siding is illegal in the state of Connecticut, which also requires green shutters on all windows of private homes.

The House Divided

The interior walls of houses used to be made of *plaster,* wonderful stuff made of lime, sand and water; some old plaster was thickened with horse-

---

4. Stucco and adobe are two forms of Real Siding popular in Hollywood, Texas and New Mexico, where the legend of Zorro is an important design inspiration.

hair. It was mixed up in great gooey batches and slapped onto thin strips of wood called *laths* to form nice, solid barriers, which retained heat in winter, stayed cool in summer and absorbed all noise. Plaster is the reason old houses feel like old houses.

A new house feels like a new house because its walls are made of sheetrock, also known as drywall, also known as plasterboard. No matter what you call it, it's awful. Concocted of gypsum, a mineral without any function or admirable properties at all, sheetrock crumbles if you drop it, warps if you bend it and dissolves if you wet it.[5] It insulates like an open window and dampens sound like a snare drum. The best thing about a house made with sheetrock is that you can operate the remote control of your television even if you're two floors away from the set.

Simply Shocking

Haywiring.

Antiquated wiring is a source of heartache and expense. Overload the system and it can burst into flame. Too few outlets and you have to festoon the place with extension cords, which collect dust and get chewed by cats. Insufficient volt-

5. Unless you use MR (moisture-resistant) Board, which is about as water repellent as your four-year-old raincoat.

age will force you to use an anemic hair dryer. Worst of all, you will eventually have to rewire the place and that costs the earth.

A house with new wiring must be "up to code." This means there are thirty-five electrical outlets in every room (including closets) except the kitchen, where there will not be enough outlets to brew coffee and make toast at the same time. The heart of a new electrical system is the *circuit breaker,* which is safer than a fuse box but cannot be used for melting pennies. A new electrical system should provide "two-hundred watt service," at the very least, which is still not quite enough to power a vacuum cleaner without plunging the house into darkness. When shopping, see if your broker knows the difference between volts and amps; a good electrical system should include plenty of both. Wattage, however, is not included in a standard residential wiring system. Homeowners must supply their own. Fortunately, wattage is readily available in light bulbs.

Fascinatin' Insulation

Insulation determines the energy efficiency of a dwelling more than any other single factor, unless the front door is missing or you're some kind of fresh-air nut who can't sleep with the windows closed. The insulating power of insulation is called its "R value," for reasons that contractors refuse to explain (see "The Lost Language of Contractors," p. 127). It is the most improbable-looking of building materials: the fiberglass variety looks like cotton candy; foam looks like marshmallow; blown-in cellulose looks like those doodads you wrap breakables in when you mail them. None of it seems very impressive, but they tell me you've got to have it.

Stay away from urea-formaldehyde insulation, though. Not only is it unhealthy, but just think of what's in it: urea and formaldehyde. Ugh.

Grace Under Water Pressure

Plumbing systems consist of two sets of pipes. One set brings water into the house and disperses it to faucets and, uh, other places. The other carries dirty water and, uh, things to the main disposal pipe, which transports waste to a septic tank or sewer line. Houses that release their wastes into cesspools should be charming and quaint in other ways too, not to mention upwind.

Plumbing crazy. Checking the plumbing fixtures requires boldness but will so impress your broker that you may come to enjoy barging into strange bathrooms, filling up the basin with hot water and clocking how long it takes to drain. Eventually you'll run through the hot water supply, and the seller's entire family will have to take cold showers.

The, uh, other things. Move now to the Big Blush. Approach the commode and smile heartily at the seller, delightedly surprised that there's a toilet there at all. Small world. Crumple up a generous length of toilet paper, drop it into the bowl and flush. When you hear the ballcock drop, cross your fingers, hold your breath and keep smiling no matter what happens.

Climate Control

It's a rule of househunting that the best heating system is the kind your broker is showing you:

Method	Broker's Pitch	Translation
Steam	"Won't dry your sinuses"	Bangs, hisses, leaks
Baseboard	"Efficient"	Breaks down with frequency of Italian car; also bangs, hisses, leaks
Hot-air ducts	"Quiet, thorough"	Drafty and stuffy at same time
Radiant heat	"Inconspicuous"	Impossible to get at when it bangs, hisses and leaks

What Do You Mean They Don't Eat Much?

If *termites* get into the structural members (see p. 62) of a house, it can be cheaper—and a lot more fun—to blow the place up and start from scratch rather than try to repair the damage. Keep this in mind when your broker advises you to go with "that discount termite service that handles all the homes in the area." Usually, however, your broker has this to say when you ask about termites:

"Good question! As far as I know, there are no termites north of the Mason-Dixon Line.
       south of the Mason-Dixon Line.
       on the Mason-Dixon Line.
       east of the Mississippi.
       west of the Mississippi.
       Of course, I'm no expert."

Termite treatment does not eliminate other insects that feed on real estate. Among these are *carpenter ants,* little fellows with thick forearms and painter's hats; true to their name, they use

---

Radon . . . and on . . . and on

Radon is a "natural" gas that is every bit as bad for you as a man-made environmental hazard. Amazing! It comes from —oh, you don't want to know where it comes from. Radon seeps into the basements and walls of homes, where people can breathe it and owners and brokers alike can deny there is any problem.

Houses with high radon levels can be made habitable by the installation of huge basement venting fans that operate around the clock. Such dwellings are particularly prized by retired sea captains who like their homes to sound like ocean liners.

houses as the raw material for carpentry, making ant-size furniture and utensils. *Powderpost beetles,* no bigger than the seeds on a Kaiser roll, can turn your house's posts into powder (a useful substitute for dust).

The Water Issue

"What water issue?"

Your broker will fend off your every attempt to find out if there is now or ever has been water damage to the house. Brokers know that, once you've bought a place, you'll come to think of water as a wayward scamp living by its own rules and occasionally wandering where it shouldn't, like the basement (see "Your Water Questions Answered," p. 108). But until then, they'll do anything at all to cover up evidence of

Water Problems

"What water problems?"

No real estate professional knows of any water problems in any home on the market.

There are no water problems.

Water caveat: Anytime you see valuable belongings such as furs and paintings in the basement, you can be sure they've been placed there to impress you. That basement floods every spring. It would be easy to prove this by popping over during a downpour, but there's no recorded instance of a prospective buyer being allowed into a house on sale during so much as a drizzle.

The Bulge Issue

"What bulge issue?"

This is what your broker will say if asked about any bulges in the wall. You will hear many interesting explanations for bulges in the wall:

◆ A racoon lived there.

◆ The house is settling into the foundation, but the walls haven't caught up yet.

◆ The paint is separating from the plaster.

Although these are all plausible reasons, none of them is true.

The Bulge Problem

Bulges in the wall are always worse than they look. This is because they're caused by moisture—or, as normal people say, water. No one knows where this moisture comes from, but it's not supposed to be there. In time, the whole house will be one irreparable waterlogged bulge.

Bulges are worse than they look. Always.

Taking Your Broker's Word for It

Listen carefully to all claims made by your broker. Ignore brazen generalities, such as "The windows are all in order." This means they exist. If, however, your broker says, "These windows are double-glazed thermal panes," get it in writing.

A Word to the Wise

Do not purchase a home that attracts you because it seems like a challenge, especially if your broker tells you to "use your imagination." A home should not be a challenge. A home should be a comfortable haven away from the many new challenges its purchase brings down upon you, such as how you're going to pay for it.

Let's Get Fiscal

Understanding Home Finance

Pay cash for your house and your broker will provide a sedan chair to take you to the closing, where everyone will be very nice. Most of us, however, need to borrow serious coin before we can afford a piece of real estate, and that's why banks become obscenely rich. Researching the home mortgage market is draining, unless you're able to discuss enormous sums of money that you'll owe for the rest of your life without becoming so addled that you can barely speak. You can regain some of your composure by reminding yourself that a home mortgage is the only form of debt that confers respectability. Racetrack habitués and compulsive shoppers are known to one and all for what they are: irresponsible bums. But take out a mortgage and you're a solid citizen. Homeowners are not *debtors*; they are *borrowers*. Vive la différence.

Your Mortgage Questions Answered

The field of home finance has changed radically in the last few years, yet the questions that borrowers ask remain fundamentally the same: Why is "mortgage" spelled with a "t" and how come the "t" isn't pronounced? The answers are simple yet revealing.

The word "mortgage" comes from Old French. "Mort" means dead; the "t" is silent because— well, try saying "t" followed by "g" a few times fast and you'll know why the "t" is silent. "Gage" means a pledge, promise or commitment. A mortgage, then, is "a promise that kills," or an obligation that haunts you until you die.

The other crucial mortgage question is how in hell to pick the right one. There are more varieties of home loans available today than at any time in history. Not a single bank employee is willing or able to explain the differences among them (see "Bankfolk," p. 83), and no normal person can figure them out unassisted. I speak as a homeowner able not only to balance his checkbook (sort of) but also to compute a waiter's tip without using scratch paper.

Take heart in the knowledge that most mortgagors can no longer remember why they succumbed to the mortgage they have or even what kind it is. All they remember is poring over pamphlets from banks and finally, exhausted, taking the mortgage some loan officer said they should.

Mortgages Demystified

Long ago, all mortgages had a fixed rate of interest. You filled out an application, groveled awhile and one day, bingo!—you got your mortgage, twenty-five or thirty years of payments that would never change. If you were lucky, your banker wore sleeve garters and called you "youngster."

Today, *fixed-rate mortgages* have the highest rates of all mortgages; this is the premium you pay for knowing that the ball to which you're chained won't get any bigger. Be careful when you receive the commitment letter for a fixed-rate mortgage. Somewhere on this document is the total amount of money, interest and principal combined, that you'll pay the bank over the term of the loan. Looking at this figure when alone can cause *mortgage vertigo*. Some applicants turn into pillars of salt.

Adjustable rate mortgages (ARMs) offer low initial interest rates, easy qualification requirements, and the laughably improbable chance that your interest rate will go down when it's adjusted, which may happen every six months, or three years, or whenever the bank feels like it. Some ARMs have adjustable rates but fixed payments, which means your debt increases even as you think you're reducing it. Sometimes ARMs have *lifetime caps* and sometimes you get slammed with *negative amortization.* Who knows what it all means? ARMs allow banks to make money in ways that no one outside their industry can even understand.

Balloon mortgages leave a substantial portion of the principal to pay off at the end of the loan; this lump sum hits you like a lead balloon.

Graduated payment or *growth equity mortgages* start with low interest rates, then get bigger and bigger so that your debt keeps pace with any success you may have later in life.

A *blended mortgage* combines several interest rates into a single payment structure. Just figuring one of these out makes you yearn for some nice *blended Scotch.* So will a *wraparound mortgage*, financed in part by the bank and in part by a seller willing to advance you money for a house if only you'll take it. A wraparound mortgage requires so much paper to state the terms of the loan that you can wrap it around yourself and save on fuel costs.

How Mortgage Interest Is Computed

Your bank officer longs to be asked how interest rates are calculated. It's a chance to show off. His posture will visibly improve while he natters on about the Prime, the Index, International Bullion

Surrogates, T-Bills and the Federal Home-Loan Mortgage Average. This talk of *stable financial indicators*, as they are called, is designed to make you believe that rational computation underlies your interest rate. Don't be naïve. Interest rates are invented by men in suits for the benefit of men in suits. Their only guide is what they feel the traffic will bear before the citizenry turns to barter or violent revolution.

Computing mortgage interest.

Conclusion

Your quest for financing will probably begin well before you come to terms on a house. The period of research is the last time anyone from a bank will ever be nice to you, so enjoy. Ask questions, listen halfheartedly, then repeat your questions as many times as you'd like. Concentrate on questions that are of no relevance, such as why banks print the APRs of their interest rates in such tiny type.[1] Shopping for money can be fun. But be prepared. Once you choose a bank and sign on the dotted line, away go the kid gloves and out come the rubber truncheons.

---

1. The *annual percentage rate* is the rate of interest you actually pay on a loan. The bank would prefer you didn't think about that.

Buddy, Can You Spare a Dime

(Repayable at 11¼% over 30 Years with a Balloon Payment Due After 7 Years)

Communist Influence at the Bank

Bank angst is caused in part by the fact that no place in the U.S.A. is more like Eastern Europe than a bank. Only here do vast numbers of red-blooded Americans wait on line for hours to talk to dawdling bureaucrats who wield immense power and don't give a damn about them. Old-fashioned banks are like the Kremlin: the murmurs of pleading customers are lost in the vaulted ceilings, drowned by heels clacking on marble floors. New banks are Kafkaesque: fluorescent lights, low-ceilinged corridors, modular furniture. All banks look as if they have ways to make you talk.

Bankers' Hours and What They Do with the Extra Time

For bankers, time is a fluid medium, expanding and contracting to suit the bank's convenience and/or whim. Bankers' hours are calculated to make the rest of us toe the line.

In the morning, banks open late enough that you're forced to watch the bank employees strolling around with their steaming coffee cups while you're dying to get in and get out so you won't be late for work. After three o'clock, when the rest of us are trying to get through the Long March of the afternoon to Happy Hour, bank employees pull down the blinds and play with your money.

Literally.

Oh, they put it all back, usually. But not before they've played Monopoly with it or pretended to light cigars with hundred-dollar bills. The atmosphere is festive, particularly if there's been no robbery that day. Bank executives feel that this "wind-down" time gives the employees a chance to work off the tensions of the day. Sometimes, the higher-ups join in, too. By four o'clock or so, everything is put away and bank employees can beat the rush hour home or catch an aerobics class.

Bankfolk

You'd think with all these opportunities to relax, bankers would be well balanced, even-tempered and easy to work with.

Well, they're not.

They are erratic, volatile and difficult. Like W.C. Fields, bank personnel would always rather be in Philadelphia. Your loan officer is likely to call three weeks after you left five messages and breezily ask if you'd mind ferreting out every credit card receipt you've acquired in the last seven years and bringing them to the bank by, say, tomorrow, so you won't have to wait through another three-month cycle to have your mortgage processed. You'll knock yourself out to find them and then the bank will take eight

Your banker wants to help.

weeks to *process your material,* whatever that may mean. Dealing with these people, you cannot win.

Help yourself by looking for the personality that occasionally glimmers through your bank person's worsted armor:

The *bank mother* is corpulent and solicitous. She explains everything slowly, encouraging you to ask questions. She really wants you to *understand* why a prepayment penalty is ethical. When she finally produces your letter of commitment, she might throw in a little chicken soup. You'll be so eager to do well by her that everything she says will float right past you. Be sure you hang on to all your pamphlets.

The *brusque, gum-snapping banker* resents you for the size of the mortgage you want. She may work on her nails while she talks to you.

Your bank mother.

The *American Gothic banker,* unique among loan officers, does not approve of lending. He treats you with a condescending hauteur suggesting that if you were living decently, within your means, you wouldn't be there trying to borrow:

YOU: So there it is. I'm virtually assured of a raise at the end of this year, which will allow me to swing the payments. And until then, there's no better collateral than my bridgework (*grinning broadly to display teeth*).

BANKER: Assured of a raise, eh? I bet that's what a lot of your yuppie friends were saying the day right before Black Monday—and how are they managing now? And how will you, my live-for-today friend? Hm?

The *dumb-as-a-post banker* is encountered more frequently than you'd expect from bank ad-

vertising. Mortgage applicants are often aston-
ished when the sobersided individuals to whom
they are forced to appeal don't know anything:

YOU: So if my payments don't pay off
the interest due on the principal,
the principal actually gets larger
without my knowing it, right?

BANKER: Looks that way, doesn't it?

YOU: But then I'll be paying more and
owing more, too. That's—oh, my
God—*negative amortization*!

BANKER: You know, that sounds familiar...

Banker Friendly

Once you actually apply for your mortgage, you
can no longer afford to be the disagreeable, queru-
lous lout you were when shopping around. You
must be courteous. Dress sensibly, but never wear
a Banker's Gray suit to a bank regardless of your
sex. Bank personnel will resent you for dressing
like one of them and may suspect you are trying to
hang around unnoticed until after closing so you
can play with the money.

Bring along as much financial background
about yourself as you can carry without using a
knapsack.[1] Cover all the bases: three years of tax
returns; four years of W-2's and 1099's, the title to

---

1. Never wear a knapsack into a bank; it is wrong, all wrong.

your car, any serious jewelry you own, and all bank statements since 1978. On a separate sheet of paper, write down your income and your spouse's, their combined total (net and gross) and the average of the two, just for the hell of it. List what you spend for rent, car payments, VCR rentals, dog-track tab, unearned income such as dividends, stock, inherited wealth, trusts, securities and lottery winnings.[2] On receipt of all this, the loan officer will hand you an application to take home and fill out, then get up to leave for lunch. Politely but forcefully, ask how quickly they can get the show on the road. The officer will shrug and say there's really not much that can be done about hurrying things along until you've done your part, so why don't you just stop blocking the door? The application will not have enough room on it to contain all the information required and you will get cramps in your hand from writing so small.

Waiting for the Dough

When you return to the bank with the completed form, your loan officer will require the same information from you all over again, this time orally. This recitation is called your *financial statement.*

Your application is then cast into the sea of tranquillity that is the bank's processing department. During this period of waiting, you'll think you're developing shingles on your knuckles. Every time you call the bank, you'll get an an-

---

2. If you have substantial winnings you're unsure what to do with, please contact me in care of the publisher.

Your financial statement.

swering machine that says the computers are down, the mortgage department is closed and please don't call back later.

Eventually your officer will answer the phone. You'll identify yourself with a lyric evocation of the friendly moment you shared when you discovered that you both love dachshunds.[3] You'll be dimly recalled after adding your salary and current debt. The officer will say your material is "in the hopper." You'll say you hope you don't lose the house. The officer will say "Hmmm."

YOU: What do you mean "Hmmm"? Will I get my approval? Before interest rates triple?

OFFICER: It's hard to say. If worse comes to worse, you can always go to the seller and beg for more time.

YOU: I already begged for more time when your office closed to redecorate.

---

3. You don't *really*, of course, but you noticed the picture of the dachshund on the officer's desk and figured what the hell.

OFFICER:	I could okay an extension of the lower rate right now, but I'm off to Tuscany and I don't have time. Someone else will—
YOU:	No! *Please* no! You know our whole situation. We'll just have to go over it all again. Please don't go, please...
OFFICER:	That's what we like to hear! Only fooling about Tuscany. We'll be right here. Now, I have a racquetball date.

The folks at your bank want to know your desire for a mortgage is sincere. Convince them of this and you'll receive a *letter of commitment* formalizing the bank's willingness to grant you a mortgage, providing no one turns against you within the next month. Although the bank commits to the loan, it does not yet *lock in* the rate at which you'll pay it back. You now buy the newspapers daily to follow interest rate fluctuations: a waste of time, really, since they only fluctuate up.

You've almost bought your house. What's left is the closing, the meeting at which ownership of the property is transferred. Like the Japanese tea ceremony, the closing is full of protocols, customs and symbolic acts. In this case, however, you'll want something stronger than tea. For it is at the closing that the legal profession comes forward, jaws dripping, to bite off its piece of the action.

Of *Course* You Need a Lawyer!

Encounters of the Wrong Kind

The closing is when the attorney's finely honed skills really come into play: putting papers into piles, handing you pens, moving paper clips around with an élan that will have all the lesser professionals assembled sighing with admiration and respect.

Hire a real estate specialist to handle your closing. Ascertaining who is a real estate lawyer is not difficult as long as you don't ask directly, in which case you will be told: "Sure I do a little real estate" or "I know something about it." This means that he or she skims the real estate section of the Sunday paper and handled the paperwork on the condo when his or her divorce came through.[1]

The attorney should work in the area of your new home. Don't believe your lawyer buddy who says, "If I can do a closing here, I can do one over there." Closing customs differ.[2] At the very least, your lawyer should know the location of the bathroom in the building where the closing is held, so you can run in and splash water on your face before starting.

Legal Fees and Your Heart

Be seated when discussing remuneration with your attorney. Falling down can add costly seconds to your time charges. Simulated heart palpitations in the lawyer's office were once a popular way to broach the subject of fee reductions, but the modern jurist is rigorously trained to spot fake symptoms.

Insist on getting the lawyer's rates in writing; this record is your best protection against reas-

---

1. See note on real estate professionals and divorce, p. 24.

2. In California you can even close without an attorney, a criminal travesty of justice which the Bar Association of the Raisin State is no doubt struggling mightily to undo.

Legal Caveat

Never hire a lawyer who offers a "special friend's rate." Remember that, to a lawyer, a friend is anyone with money. The "friend's rate" is always more than you think, especially if you forgot to ask for it in writing (see *"taking a shot,"* below). To add insult to penury, your lawyer friend will almost certainly screw up at the closing and expect you to forgive and forget because, after all, he was doing you a favor, and besides, what do you want for the special friend's rate?

---

sessed charges based on unforeseen additional expenses, cost of living increases or the time-honored lawyer's custom called *taking a shot.* Ask directly what the charges are to do a closing, and the lawyer will be so surprised that you might get a discount—but it's not very likely.

Lawyers charge in one of three ways:

À la carte: separate charges for individual services such as organizing title search, blinking, crossing legs, etc. These add up, and the itemized bill is impressive, almost as if the lawyer has been busy on your behalf.

By the hour: results in client paying for lawyer's coffee breaks, fights with wife, calls concerning own stock portfolio, etc.

Flat fee: usually a percentage of the cost of the home; permits linkage of lawyer's take to value of dwelling on principle that client who is buying a costly home can afford to be gouged one more time.

What Your Lawyer Does for All That Money

◆ Reviews all the papers your broker wants you to sign.[3]

◆ Collects all documents required for closing in a safe place where they won't be packed or thrown out with the trash, in which case the closing will have to be postponed while you run around collecting duplicates and the lawyer charges more.

◆ Leaves a *paper trail* showing that you knew what you thought you were doing was what you intended to do, and that you think you intended to have all the right documentation to prove it. Probably.

◆ Takes care of obtaining title insurance, which you should be grateful for because who knows what it is or where you go to get it.

◆ Prepares a *closing statement,* the record of who paid what to whom in exchange for what. Don't pay your attorney until you receive your closing statement; they all try to put off preparing them in hopes that clients will forget and no wonder. Dull, dull, dull!

---

3. Make sure your attorney understands them; unfortunately, this requires hiring another lawyer to quiz the one you already have.

Be Sure You Bring a Lot of Checks

The Closing

You *can* close on a property without actually attending a closing. At an *escrow closing,* an *escrow agent* assembles all the documentation and checks required, then sits at a large table and moves from chair to chair, playing the roles of buyer, seller, realtor, etc. Escrow agents wear many hats (sometimes literally, just for the fun of it). Escrow closings are perfectly legal, but why miss an experience as thrilling as your own closing? A closing is something you'll remember forever, like the night you threw up at the prom.

I remember my closing well. The sellers, previously a solicitous, nervously smiling couple who lurked in the background during my visits to the house, sat across from me, glowering. The broker hulked around like an expectant father. My lawyer closed his *Sports Illustrated* and opened the manila envelope containing papers I'd moved heaven and earth to get to him in time for this event. Yawning, he began to read them.

Now?

Shouldn't he have looked them over in advance? I cast an inquiring glance his way, more a crazed rolling of the eyeballs, actually. "No problem," he said, fixing me with that calm, reassuring look they teach them in law school. I did not know at the time he was speaking for himself. Nor did I know that the surveyor's report indicated that the lot the house sits on was less than I'd been told.[1] Nor did I know the inspector who'd okayed the place was related to my broker by marriage.

All I knew was that if I signed enough papers and checks, the house I craved would soon be mine. And so I did. I signed and signed and signed, and sure enough, the house was mine, no problem.

The problems came later.

---

1. The broker's "ballpark estimate" (a real estate term meaning *lie*) was within 10 percent of the actual dimensions of the land—shabby but, after all, a broker's no expert.

Who Are Those Guys, Anyway?
The Cast of the Closing

The point of the closing is to transfer ownership (the *title*) of the dwelling from seller to buyer. Your closing can run you as much as 8 percent of the cost of the house. Even worse, the event requires you to spend hours surrounded by people you'd just as soon avoid.

Today you envy the *seller,* that clod who's getting who knows how much over market value for that house. Closings are frequently family affairs for the seller, so don't be surprised if you find yourself facing a united front. They're all going out afterward for a lovely meal, paid for with money you're about to fork over. Still they look at you balefully, as if you're dispossessing them.

The *lawyers* are usually the only people at the closing with tans. Buyers' and sellers' attorneys often know each other. If they're getting paid by the hour, they'll ask about each other's kids and make small talk. If they're not, they'll get right down to business. Occasionally, lawyers will flare up and scream about things like the cost of a sixteenth of a tank of fuel. The more niggling the bone of contention, the more ferocious their fussing. This is called the *lawyers' minuet.*

The *bank representative* will not be the same functionary who ballyhooed mortgages to you, nor the sallow Pilgrim who made you provide a blood sample for your credit appraisal. This bank representative is plumper and more senior, like Charles Laughton in *Mutiny on the Bounty* or an aging

KGB agent.[2] This official will turn over the mortgage to you and collect such fees as the bank is
entitled to receive: starting fees, discount points,
and a contribution to the Bank Tellers' Widows
Fund. The bank representative wants everybody
to hurry up so the closing doesn't cut into break
time.

The persistent sound of knuckles drumming
on the table top comes from the hands of the
broker, there to collect his or her commission from
the seller. Eschewing the tiresome custom of bill-
ing by mail for services, real estate brokers demand payment right there at closing, a vivid
demonstration of the dignity and unhurried grace
that distinguish their profession. At my closing,
the broker was visibly salivating; it was so unsettling that my lawyer looked up from his *TV Guide*
as he planned his weekend while waiting for me to
finish up. Stick around and watch the sellers pay
the broker if you can. It's one of the few checks
you're not writing.

The *title closer* is a total stranger without
whom nothing can proceed. The closer checks and
ensures the title, issues it to you and records the
deed at the county courthouse. Your lawyer will
whisper to you that you might slip this functionary a twenty[3] to make sure the deed is properly
filed. Who knows if this is necessary? Maybe the
lawyer gets half.

---

2. See "Communist Influence at the Bank," p. 81.

3. Perhaps a fifty by the time you read this.

Why a Title Search?

The purpose of a title search is to make sure there are no *defects* in the title—like a *lien.* A lien is a claim on property. Clear up any liens on the house before you find them leaning on you. An *easement* is the legal right of one party to use the property of another. Make sure the seller is not retaining the right to use your linen closet or have people over to watch the Super Bowl in your den.

Be Prepared

Bring a good pen and practice your signature the night before. At the closing, you and the seller are both called *principals,* in order to make things less confusing for the lawyers.

Your lawyer, by the way, should remind you to bring checks. Mine didn't. I had to borrow blank ones from the bank and it was extremely embarrassing, not that I'm bitter. A normal person as-

Practice your signature the night before.

sumes that paying for a house is like paying for anything else: you hand over a check and that, my friend, is that. For a house, you write checks for the loan origination fee, appraisal fee, credit report, lender's inspection fee, mortgage insurance application fee, first interest payment, mortgage insurance premium, hazard insurance premium, reimbursement for expenses now assumed by you such as water bills or taxes, pest inspection fee, government recording and transfer charges, survey and title insurance premium and miscellaneous contingencies. Oh, and don't forget a certified check for the house. That's key. Got that?[4]

Let the Revels Begin

Endorse the back of the certified check over to the seller and sign your own check for the down payment. Hand both checks to your attorney, who will hand them to the seller's attorney. They will smile at each other conspiratorially; a nervy few will lick their chops. The seller's attorney hands the checks to—

Stop! Stop! You Forgot to Visit the House Before Closing!

No one will like you for this, but you'd better take a peek at the place just before you close. At best,

---

4. You could have found all this out the day before by looking over a Uniform Settlement Statement, an itemized list of all your closing charges. But you have to know to ask, and who the hell ever heard of such a thing?

you'll be underfoot while people are trying to pack. At worst, you'll find some previously hidden problem that could delay the closing if not blow the deal altogether.

Your contract states that the house must be left in a *broom-clean state*. Bring along a small whisk broom and check a corner or two. The sellers will respect your thoroughness even while wishing you a slow, wasting death. They may also remove every single last light bulb and pour bacon grease down the drain just to be cute.

Make sure the sellers take their stuff, including their garbage—especially their garbage. Make sure they take their pets, too; some homeowners pull up stakes just to get away from them.

You can now safely say that you've done all a mortal being can do to avert disaster in your new home.

Let the Revels Resume

The seller hands you the deed. Hands are shaken all around. Congratulations. This land is your land.

Part Three:

Making It Your Own

Packing It In

A Moving Experience

Social scientists tell us that the stress of moving is equal to that of divorce, loss of a loved one or getting fired. What do social scientists know? Moving is much worse.

Moving requires that you lay out the accumulated debris of your life and bundle it into parcels. You entrust this precious cargo to muscular strangers who'll charge you a fortune and break your most precious possessions. Then, just when the stress of packing begins to abate, it's time to unpack.

Timing Is Everything

There are two ways to pack, each with distinct disadvantages:

◆ Stretch the process out over several weeks, packing a few cartons each day. All the comforts of home will dwindle around you, and your children will become cranky and depressed because you packed their Nintendo set in the first carton.

◆ Leave it until the last minute, stay up for days and go to your closing exhausted and unkempt. Later, you'll discover that in all the commotion you threw out your great-grandmother's gold lorgnette.

The Art of Packing

Be selective. This is a good time to streamline your belongings. For example:

Throwaways: Dozens of bottles of ancient, dried-up spices from the back of the top shelf of the kitchen cabinet.

Keepers: Shoeboxes full of letters from people you never told your spouse about.[1]

The only place that has the right-size cartons for packing is the liquor store. You'll feel obligated

---

1. You may be tempted to look up some of these people in the phonebook just for the hell of it. Don't be a fool.

to buy something out of sheer embarrassment, so include the price of a half-gallon of light rum in your moving costs. A parade of liquor boxes into your home is just the way to create a good impression on your new neighbors.

Pack heavy or breakable objects in the center of each carton and surround them with soft items to provide cushioning. You'll run out of underwear long before you run out of coffee mugs; this will disquiet you. Label your cartons with the initials of the rooms you want them to end up in, but don't expect the movers to be able to read your handwriting or even look at it. At least your underwear will be all over the house.

For little more than you paid your lawyer, you can have the movers pack for you. The upside of this arrangement is that movers don't waste hours looking at your high school yearbook; they sling everything in

You can never have too many cartons.

cartons, stick it in their truck and drive off. Be sure you point out to them all living beings—plant, animal or child—that could be mistaken for packables.

Movers and Shakers

The moving business is a cultural hodgepodge: Santini Brothers, Moishe the Mover, O'Reilly's Overland. Some movers are careerists who've been lifting and driving for years, some work part-time to support careers as avant-garde playwrights, but they have two things in common: the upper-body strength of a derrick and a resistance to hernia. Considering what a vulnerable situation you're in when they converge on you, movers as a whole are remarkably honest[2] even though one member of the team will always loiter disturbingly around your stereo equipment. Keep tabs on your wallet at all times. It'll be hard to forget about anyway, as it will be bulging with the cash in which movers insist on being paid. Before you hand over the wad, though, poke through a few cartons authoritatively, checking for breakage, then pay.

The moving men will not move.

You forgot their tip. They didn't.

After the moving men have gone, relax for a few minutes in the midst of the clutter. *Breathe.* Smell the smell of your new house. Savor the *moment.* Take a snapshot.

Now you have to unpack.

Divorce, death and getting fired just can't compare.

---

2. A crew of lawyers in the same circumstances would probably make off with your storm windows.

I Think I've Made a Terrible Mistake

Rude Awakenings

No matter how many times you visited or how carefully the inspector inspected, you can never really *know* a house until you inhabit it. Only then do you discover the features that will cause you to smack yourself on the forehead and your friends to point out that no one held a knife to your throat when you bought the place. Cheer up. Within a few years, you should be able to sell for enough to make back most of your closing costs.

In the meantime, you'd better learn to cope.

Your Water Questions Answered

A contractor I know is fond of saying, "Water is, like, really, the most amazing thing, you know?"[1] How right he is.

Water problems are of two sorts: no water where you need it to be, or plenty where you would prefer it weren't. Any ponds, streams or decorative falls on your property will dry up within two weeks of closing even if it's the rainy season. On the other hand, the bog-like puddle in the yard that your broker said was "left from last month's big storms" will turn out to be seepage from your septic tank.

Water doesn't really do much, unlike wood, which can warp, bend, rot, snap, crack or burn, or metal, which can rust, corrode, twist or disintegrate. Water can only stand or run. Standing water looks like it's just lying there. Running water is likely to slow to a crawl shortly after you move in, and you'll need to get your pump fixed.

The land around your house should be *graded* carefully so that water runs away from the dwelling. Water that doesn't run away from your house will go and stand in your basement. Unfortunately, your neighbors may have graded *their*

---

1. Note use of complete sentence, indicating prep school background. See also *"Hippy Carpenter,"* p. 119.

land, too, so that their water runs away from their house—over toward your house. The result? Someone else's water standing in your basement.

The first time you go down there and see six murky inches of loitering moisture, you'll become curious about your *water table*, which is what all the water around your house is standing on. Sometimes the water standing on the table will suddenly jump up, right into your basement. Water that jumps is called *sump*. You remove sump with a *sump pump*. I have a real fondness for my sump pump because it turns on and off automatically so I don't have to learn how.

Hard water is so called because it's hard to work up a good lather with it when you're washing your hair. Hard water tastes as if someone's been soaking Revereware in it and leaves furry deposits on the inside of your tea kettle. The fibrous particles that come out of your faucets are caused by the same mineral buildup. Probably. If they were asbestos, or anything bad like that, your water analysis would have shown it.

You did have a water analysis, didn't you?

Soft water makes lather that is impossible to wash out of your hair. Usually, it tastes as if it comes from a swimming pool.

Speaking of swimming pools, have cracks started to appear through the fresh paint on the bottom? What's that hole in the ground do to your premiums? How come your pool attracts everyone else's dead leaves?

Summary of Conclusions. Water is, like, really, the most amazing thing, you know?

Critters

Owners of homes on the market usually get their wildlife to go into hiding with the understanding that they stay and torment the next residents.

Roaches. In parts of the South, roaches are so tough you have to hit them with a hammer to do any damage. My roaches are less hearty, but so nimble that they seem to be rehearsing the "Dance at the Gym" from *West Side Story* every time I turn on the kitchen light. You can control your roaches, but don't expect them to relinquish their title to your house. They're indigenous.

Waterbugs look like roaches writ large; in fact, they're as big as small dogs. In Florida waterbugs are called *palmetto bugs,* and they can fly—often into your iced tea. Happily, waterbugs are transients, always moving on, probably en route to Florida to take flying lessons.

Bats. One-quarter of the warmblooded mammals in the world are bats, so it's no wonder you've got some in your attic. Bats don't live where you can see them. They squeeze into out-of-the-way perches in the eaves or your attic crawlspace. You'll notice your bats the first time you stand outside admiring the way your house looks in the twilight. Suddenly zip, zip, zip—bats will be circling the place like old-time barnstormers. Most homeowners are terrified of bats, but they should

loosen up. After all, bats do not fly into your hair (at least not often) or suck your blood (ever). Bats eat the insects that would otherwise engulf you during the summer months. Most important, they're not rodents (see "Rodents," below).

Reptiles. In southern climes, homes come equipped with little lizards that slither around so fast you're never really sure they're there. These are the maximum-size reptiles you should allow near your home. Larger reptiles like *frogs*, *turtles* or *snakes* indicate a moisture problem. In Florida, where there's a lot of moisture, some homeowners have been surprised, and even eaten up, by *alligators* right on their front lawns.

Rodents. Cheer up. You'll never have a *rat* and *mouse* infestation simultaneously. They don't negotiate. Either the rats eat the mice, or the mice drive the rats crazy and they leave. Mice are not nearly as unsettling as rats. Field mice are sweet, actually, if you have the mind of a child. Rats are another matter. Check the inspection report for

---

Toad Note

Toads may drop into your basement if there's a lot of rain outside. These warty little rapscallions are self-conscious and shy because of the bad press they receive in children's books. But they're harmless and really sort of cute. Only a cad would exterminate his toads. Take them outside and bid them au revoir.

any mention of rat infestation. Check the Yellow Pages for a pest-control service that makes emergency calls. Then check into a motel. Rats! How could you have bought a place with rats!

Neighbors

We all want our new neighbors to be like Spring Byington in *December Bride*, popping over to greet us the day we arrive with a pert smile, a lilting "Hi there, neighbor!" and some piping-hot cherry cobbler.

It's more likely, however, that you'll meet your neighbors when their dog bites you.

You should have made sure before buying that the house was not next door to a religious cult that begins chanting the minute the sun comes up. But you couldn't have known about the lumpy, hideous youths across the way until their heavy-metal band started tuning up for nightly practice. Other neighbors' customs unlikely to be discovered until it's too late include:

◆ Keeping goats
◆ Setting up an enormous Christmas display on the roof that draws tourist buses
◆ Ironmongering

Local Developments

Remember when I said you should attend a town meeting before settling into a community? You didn't, did you? So now look:

◆ The former Grange Hall just down the road
has been bought by a consortium of Hell's Angels,
who plan to use it as a regional headquarters and
detox center.

◆ Your house is beneath a flight path out of
the local commuter airport, which has just begun
to accommodate supersonic planes. As a concilia-
tory gesture, the airline offers earplugs on request
to all homeowners affected.

◆ Due to extensive roadwork scheduled for
completion in 1994, your street is an official Inter-
state detour.

Delusory Enthusiasm and Aftermath

Within weeks of moving, depression gives way to
optimism; this is the human brain's way of lying to
itself. You make notes, draw up long lists, and
walk around the house muttering, "It'll be great!
It'll be just what we want!" This frantic heartiness
will fade once you actually set about seeing what
you need to do to protect your *investment,* a term
used by homeowners who can't say *home* without
weeping. You're about to enter the realm of the
builders: contractors and subcontractors. This
hearty breed stands ready to turn your dreams
into reality and your capital improvements budget
into beer money.

Spilt Milk

Fixing It Up

Divide all defects in your home into *fixable* and *chronic* ones. Fixables are manageable. Chronics are the ones you should have thought about before you bought. But don't worry. The line between chronic and fixable is extremely vague. Most of the problems in your home will be *chronically fixable*, which means you can almost get rid of them providing you pay and pay and pay. Dealing with chronically fixable problems is called *home maintenance*.

The Three R's

Renovation is serious. It involves the replacement or rebuilding of major systems (such as the wiring) or rooms (such as the kitchen). Renovation is always time-consuming, disruptive and much more expensive than you thought it would be. A *repair* solves a limited problem (such as the wiring or the kitchen). Repairs are always time-consuming, disruptive and much more expensive than you thought they would be. Repairs are serious. *Restoration* is the complete re-creation of what a house was like at an earlier time, not only in terms of appearance but also in the materials and type of construction used. Homeowners involved in restoration never talk about the cost because it's embarrassing. Ordinary homeowners are well advised to steer clear of restoration, though some dabble (see "Newelpost Disease," p. 139).

Home improvements involve an addition to or the modernization of something in your dwelling. Most home improvements are repairs that turn into renovations, replacements or worse.

What's wrong with this picture?

If the repair you need is not too serious, should you try to fix it yourself? No, and there are good reasons why you shouldn't:

♦ You won't know what you're doing.

♦ You won't do the job well because you lack the proper tools.

♦ You won't know what you're doing.

♦ You'll hate what you're doing, and the memory will forever be a blight on the enjoyment of your home.

♦ You won't know what you're doing.

Of course, if you're going to live in a house, *some* basic manual skills are essential. I'm a bit of a Mr. Fix-It myself (see *"me as Mr. Fix-It,"* p. 58), and on weekends I'm always around the house changing light bulbs, cleaning the soap dish and folding laundry. For harder jobs, however, I seek professional help.

Contractors, the National Economy and You

Choosing a *contractor* is the first step toward making your home beautiful—well, bearable. The contractor supervises and coordinates work on your dwelling. He subcontracts with the specialized artisans, such as roofers and masons, who would snigger in your face if you tried to tell them what you want in your own words. The contractor is so called because you contract with him to do work on your home. The term is all the more appropriate because dealing with the contractor makes your stomach muscles contract.

When the Dow is strong, interest rates are down and unemployment is low. Lots of people buy houses then, and business is good for the contractor. On the other hand, when the economy is weak, people refrain from new home purchases. Instead they fix up the ones they have, so business is good for the contractor.

In winter, many contractors do not work at all; they hibernate in Gstaad, migrate to Majorca, or just stay home and work on their cars. In summer, their commitments extend years into the future, the way Luciano Pavarotti's do. In short, your contractor needs your business like he needs a third nostril.

Getting in Touch

Reaching your contractor can be tough.

All contractors maintain defective telephone answering machines that ignore calls, garble messages or cause your handset to emit a piercing busy signal even when you *know* your contractor is there.

By the time contact is made, you'll understand that the contractor works for you at his (or, in a very small number of cases, her) own leisure. Your money pays for his time, but all aggravation, frustration and gastric acidity that arise on the job are shared equally by both of you.

Warning: Even the most good-hearted contractor will not consider returning your call until
you start to experience chest pains. Many homeowners become so flummoxed when they hear
their contractor's voice on the wire that they forget entirely why they'd left fourteen messages in
the first place. Unscrupulous contractors will use
this *window of discombobulation* to convince you
of the need for pointless extravagances, like gold-
plated door hinges. Do not fall for this.

Keep calm, take a few deep breaths and tell
the contractor to hold the phone while you get
your notes. With any luck, he won't hang up.

The Varieties of Contractors

In the sixties, the American home became a
better-crafted, more karmically integrated structure thanks to the *Hippy Carpenter*. As he grew
older, the Hippy Carpenter took business courses
at night or utilized the expensive education he'd
received at places like Exeter, Reed, Bard or Cor-
nell; he incorporated and bought insurance. The
Hippy Contractor is a Hippy Carpenter with a
pocket calculator.

The Hippy Contractor is considerate and will
commiserate with you even as he explains why the
breakdown of the boiler is neither his fault nor
covered by the guarantee. His compassion extends
to the natural world, too. If work on your home
stops for a day and a half while the crew ex-
tricates a nest full of newly hatched chicks
that your contractor found halfway down your

chimney, make sure you're not billed for the time.

The Hippy Contractor has strange eating habits. He is vegetarian or macrobiotic. He can tell you which brands of canned soup contain the fewest preservatives. But bear with this lunacy. He's the easiest contractor to talk to, especially if you don't catch him when he's meditating.

The *Good-Old-Boy-with-Truck* is the local contractor who, like the local real estate agent (see "Good-Old-Boy-with-Sedan," p. 23), grew up right around where you now live and remembers what it was like before people like you started moving in and spoiling everything.

Good-Old-Boy.

This home-grown builder talks down to all his clients. He wears a baseball cap and a T-shirt with his cigarettes rolled up in a sleeve. He has sideburns and a potbelly. His habitual expression is one of contemptuous amusement, probably caused by something you've just said. The Good-Old-Boy contractor understands more about your home than you ever will, and he does not want to hear anything from you. No matter how straightforward or well-intentioned your inquiries, they'll be met with a pained stare and a few grunts.

Resist the impulse to draw out your local contractor. He may do fine work for reasonable prices, but he's a terrible conversationalist:

YOU: We were wondering what kind of siding would be most appropriate for the house...

G.O.B.: If I were you, I'd put up vinyl siding. You never have to paint it. You can wash your house with your hose.

YOU: Wouldn't clapboard be more appropriate?

G.O.B.: If I were you, I'd put up vinyl siding. You never have to paint it. You can wash your house with your hose.[1]

The *Ethnic Contractor*, drawn to the construction business because the pay is good and you don't often get asked for your Green Card, is usually the spokesman for a family from some far-off land. In New York City, there are Pakistani and Jamaican contractors; in Texas, there are Mexicans. Italian contractors

Contractor from parts unknown.

are everywhere and are famous for brooking no truck.

Be sure you communicate your wishes very specifically to the Ethnic Contractor, or you may wind up with an alternative that is just as good—but only if you live in Albania. Always be ex-

---

1. By contrast, the Hippy Contractor will grow sullen at the mention of Fake Siding (see p. 66), mumbling only that he's "not into vinyl."

tremely polite; you never know how you may be giving offense or what he'll do to get even.

Note: *Female Contractors* exist in small numbers. All Female Contractors have good hair and do graduate work in archaeology. During the summer months, the busiest season for builders, the Female Contractor departs for a dig near Fishbourne, leaving in charge her lumbering dullard of an assistant who draws an hourly wage for as long as the job takes.

The Builder's Car

When you see what your contractor drives, you'll be glad you didn't hire him as a mechanic.

The Once-and-Future Hippy's car is a crumbling compact whose windows are always open so the doors can be tied shut with string. Beneath the rusting hood, however, the engine ticks as steadily as a Swiss watch; the Hippy Contractor loves to tinker. Show some interest in automotive repair, and he'll be explaining the internal combustion engine before you can say Kahlil Gibran.

The Good-Old-Boy-with-Truck's truck has a rifle mount against the rear windshield, fuzzy dice

You can tell a lot about a contractor by what he drives.

The multipurpose truck.

hanging from the mirror, and bumper stickers opposing gun control and abortion. None of the bulging cartons, greasy machinery or lengths of pipe in the back of the truck has any relation to you. That widget you need is still on order, but if you ask nicely the G.O.B. will show you the nudie magazines he keeps in the glove compartment.

Ethnic Contractors drive vehicles belonging to other family businesses, so don't be surprised when the bluestone for your patio arrives in a mini-van bearing the name of a bakery.

Through the Nose: Payment Pitfalls

Your contractor will charge you for his services in one of two ways: by a fixed bid or on a time-and-materials basis. A fixed bid induces feelings of despair and rage, while paying time-and-materials causes sleeplessness and free-floating anxiety.

A fixed bid allows for every conceivable worst case, including nuclear winter. Still, unless you trust your contractor as much as, say, your brain surgeon, a fixed bid is the only way to protect yourself. Should you engage a contractor on a time-and-materials basis, be sure an *upset figure* is written into your agreement. This is the cost beyond which you and the contractor have agreed that it is all right for you to get upset.

Sweat equity: a poor investment.

Sweat Equity

You may want to pitch in and help the crew in a fruitless attempt to staunch the money hemorrhage. This is called *sweat equity*, a handy term with which to oppress the guests at your housewarming (see Appendix III, p. 150). Practitioners of sweat equity are motivated by nostalgia for high school shop. They try to fit in smoothly with the crew. Some go so far as to borrow overalls and John Deere caps. They hammer their thumbs and strain their backs with only the occasional trip to the emergency room to break the monotony. They end up doing a lot of sweeping and wondering how much they dare knock off the bill. Contractors hate sweat equity.

Scene of the Crime

When your contractor goes through your house, he'll act as if he alone stands between you and your home collapsing around your ears, probably when you've just gotten out of the shower and are

both wet and naked. He will inveigh against every other builder who's ever laid a hand on the place.

Yet, for all his bluster, the contractor is a diplomat when it comes to explaining what's wrong. He knows that vividness, not accuracy, is what strikes fear in a homeowner's heart:

---

15 Ways to Call Your Home a Ruin

"What's holding it up?"

"Didn't you have it inspected?"

"Boy, you're lucky I got here when I did."

"Was this the only house you could afford?"

"You a do-it-yourselfer or what?"

"Well, it has nice lines."

"The shell[2] looks sound."

"The land is worth something, I guess."

"Don't worry, in ten years you'll look like a genius."

"You must really love this place."

"I'd rather not sit inside while we talk."

"Was that a shift in the earth's crust?"

"You could fix it up bit by bit, I suppose, but you risk losing the structural members."

"I know that realtor. He's done this to a number of people in this area."

---

2. Contractors love to call your house "the shell." It makes you want to slap them.

Figure 1
Your sketch
(of a light
switch)

Figure 2
Contractor's sketch
(light switch, side
view, crumpled
paper)

Figure 3
Contractor's sketch
(light switch,
aerial view)

Visual Aids

One picture is worth a thousand words, especially when your contractor is talking. The best way to be sure you understand each other is with a simple sketch, but do not depend on the contractor's drafting skills. At heart, all contractors are abstract expressionists, working with stubby pencils or gummy ball-point pens exclusively. They don't use square pieces of paper, either, not when they can use the margin of your newspaper, an embossed dinner napkin or a soggy tatter of paper towel.

Notate these sketches carefully. They are the only records you'll have of what it was you wanted the contractor to do. Make sure your contractor indicates which sketches are overhead views and which are side views. Nothing is recognizable from these vantages, but don't mention this; your contractor will become upset, which can only mean further delay.

The Lost Language of Contractors

Examine a length of two-by-six lumber and you'll notice that it isn't two by six at all. It was once, but it was milled at the lumberyard and now it's smaller, about one and a half inches by five and a half. Roughly. Give or take. Contractor Talk is full of such distortion and mystification.

Your contractor speaks.

When the contractor refers to a plank as a two-by-six, he's implying that he wouldn't have shaved the damn thing so thin if he'd gotten his hands on it before those jerks at the mill did. The contractor refers to things as they are meant to be. This is why he refers to your drafty vestibule as the "airlock" and may even call your living room the "formal parlor."

Contractor Talk is not to be confused with Architect Speak, although each borrows freely from the other and both are equally incomprehensible (see "Do You Need an Architect?" p. 132). The contractor is an idealist, but the architect just loves to talk funny. What you refer to as a "closet" your contractor will describe as a "storage area," while your architect will, with a perfectly straight face, refer to it as a "keeping room." It's hard not to like architects for saying things like that.

Normal English	Contractor Talk	Architect Speak
Doorway	Post-and-lintel opening	Portal
Hall	The stretch with no windows	Circulation link
Window	Six-over-six double-hung thermal-panes	Fenestration option
Bumpy walls	Stucco finish	Texture treatment
Rec room	Paneled basement	Collection point
Bathroom	Your tub and your sink, and, uh, so on[3]	The brown zone
There's a flood downstairs!	It's been a wet spring	Moisture is migrating toward the sump

The urge to speak your contractor's language will grow as the rubble mounts. Resist. *Jargon envy* is an insidious addiction for which there is no satisfaction. Each foray into the Lost Language of Contractors will be met with amusement. Your contractor, noticing your use of words learned from him, will up the ante:

---

3. Contractors are modest to the point of prudery—until your back is turned.

YOU:	Well, I guess with the vapor barrier in place behind the sheathing, we'd better make some other provision for ventilation in the attic.
CONTRACTOR:	Yeah? What do you think we should use? We got louvered gable end vents, soffit vents—
YOU:	Wait! Uh—soffit vents? I like the sound of those.
CONTRACTOR:	Yeah? You like 'em plugged or perforated?
YOU:	What's the dif—
CONTRACTOR:	You should also consider turban vents, mushroom vents, vent-a-ridge, vent-a-flashing, and probably we ought to think about using some Propervent styrene spacers to ensure airflow between the rafter gaps. What d'ya say?
YOU:	Oh, you decide.

When You Think You're Losing It

From time to time, you'll be unable to fathom what in the world your contractor is talking about. Stay calm and ride it out; fake some terms if you can. Eventually it will come back to you.

Contractor: "If we keep the pediments simple, no beveling on the corners, no volutes on the facing, then we can do the porch for less than twice the original estimate. Not bad, eh?"

Improper tool storage #1.

Do not say: "The pediment is the thing on the bottom, right? And why no beveling? I like beveling. What is beveling, anyway? Twice the estimate? Oh, Christ."

Instead say: "Simple pediments, huh? I think I like that. Now, where's the drawing? (*Flip through little paper scraps with contractor's drawings on them.*) Twice the estimate? Oh, Christ."

Improper tool storage #2.

Or better: "Well, if the edges aren't beveled, why use the interlocked facing boards? Do we really need them? Christ, twice the estimate is a lot over, even for you."

You and your contractor must understand each other, particularly if you're about to have *major work* done. Major work means there will be a whole crew at your home all day. In the evening, they'll leave behind their tools, a great deal of dust and many empty soda cans. Learn to live with it. When major work is being done, your house is no longer just your house; even you will call it "the job."

A Site Is Not a Home

Big Jobs

A patient undergoing surgery is not a pretty sight; neither is a house that is being reno-vated. Parts of both that should be out of sight gape open. Normal circulation slows down and in some cases comes to a full stop. The advantage of surgery over renovation is that you're anaesthetized while it's going on.

When the contractor operates on your home,

all sensation is heightened, like during wartime. You'll wake up to the noises of power equipment, portable radios and undeleted expletives. You'll come home to the lingering aromas of tar, wood shavings and the ineffable piquancy of working men. Dust will settle on your head as you sleep; mud will scuff your shoes even when you're not wearing them.

Renovation is hell. Expect to eat out a lot while it's going on.

Do You Need an Architect?

Residential architects believe that a well-ordered, harmonious living space is conducive to a well-ordered, harmonious life. They also believe in the Tooth Fairy. Architects are not well liked. Contractors resent their authority; homeowners mistrust their pretensions, not to mention their expense. Like most professionals, architects work the cost of their schooling into their hourly rates, with cost-of-living increases added on every fifteen minutes.

Still, architects are very natty on the whole and virtually the only professionals in the world who can use the word "clerestory" in a sentence (see "Architect Speak," p. 128). If you're planning to build a home from scratch, you would do well to consult an architect (if only for a few laughs). For not much more than the cost of a Caribbean vacation for twelve, you can spend a few hours at a *program meeting* discussing your residential dreams. Perhaps you've always wanted a bidet

with views or a conversation pit (whatever happened to conversation pits?). To memorialize your chat, the architect will make up a nice sheaf of drawings on lovely thin tissue paper. With any luck there'll be little stick figures of you and your family in them, lounging around your beautiful home.

Try to find a shrink who'll do that for the same money.

Getting the Contractor There

Just as a star lets anticipation mount before emerging from the dressing room, so a contractor never shows up for work when you think he will. Contractors prefer to ooze into a job, working on your home a few hours a week before moving to another site. This cursory presence turns into a full-scale occupation as the job nears completion, then tails off again just as you're reaching the end of your rope (see "Contractor's Withdrawal," p. 140).

Ask your contractor for his home address and telephone number "so you can reach him in case of emergency." Your contractor will be reluctant to part with these, as the only emergency that would mean anything to him would be if you ran out of checks and he knows you wouldn't call about that. Insist on the information. A couple I know pulled up in front of their contractor's home every morning at five-thirty, honking furiously. While my friends' lark did not amuse the contractor, he finished two weeks ahead of schedule.

Keeping Tabs

Don't hang around the crew when they're working. They're a temperamental bunch. If they suspect you of suspecting them of stealing or goofing off, they very well might—just to retaliate. Do not

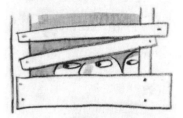

It's not nice to snoop.

under any circumstances show up with a few six-packs and a dumb grin. You will not be welcomed into the warm fraternity of these horny-handed sons of toil. They'll talk with you and drink your beer, then after you've gone they'll make fun of you, especially if you're a woman.

Stay in touch with your contractor through regularly scheduled meetings. He will show up if you make it clear that this is when you plan to pay. Serve coffee at these meetings, not beer. If you're feeling friendly, offer half-and-half.

Contractor Channeling

Contractors love to sign their work. They write their initials or their names or nasty things about you all over the house, but only where no one but another contractor can find them: on the back of sheetrock or inside the lip of the chimney. To the contractor, this is a way of speaking to colleagues of the future. To the homeowner, the custom is a completely unwarranted defacement of personal property and ought to be actionable.

This heiroglyph of a man named Amnon the Stoneshlepper was found on the wall of the burial chamber of the tomb of Ptolemy the Nicely Furnished. It was discovered only when cracks near the pinnacle of the pyramid suggested that the granite needed repointing. Workmen were sent in to see if there was any water in the sarcophagus.

Construction Gridlock

Sometimes the work just stops. Probably there's a clear explanation and no cause for concern— unless the weather changes or everybody's left for another job.

Here are the usual reasons:

Waiting for subcontractors. The electricians show up before the plumbers. The phone man shows up before the electricians. Have a drink and look in again in a few days.

Inhuman error. The wrong windows are delivered. By the time the right ones come, you have to track down the authorized window installers again, without whom the guarantee is invalid. After a number of unreturned phone calls, you say the hell with it and give the job to the contractor himself, who assures you he's installed many windows that are very similar, almost. Later, damp spots will appear around the window trim.

Safety first. At the last minute, the crew refuses to carry the extra-long tub into the bathroom because they're not sure the floor is strong enough. *The floor isn't strong enough?* You and the contractor look in the basement. You both agree that the beam looks perfectly sound and the guys are acting like a bunch of old women, but *just to be on the safe side* you decide to install a lally-column (maybe two) as well as additional bracing for the joists under the tub. The cost: "Whatever—just time and materials." You nod and sigh. Whatever.

One day you find no dumpster blocking the driveway. Inside, a gaping wound of wood and wiring is now a wall. Your house is beginning to heal. Soon it will be all better.

But not quite.

Saying Uncle

Finishing Touches

The Coming of the Painters

Everyone is glad when it's time for the painters, because everyone knows what it is they do.

Painters hate it when you point at the sunset and say, "I want the house to look like that patch of off-gold there where the cloud is, but a little less beigy." Keep your choices simple. Custom-mixed colors cost a fortune, and only you will know your house is the precise half-shade between Macaroon Bisque and Clotted Whey.

When selecting colors with spouse or family, expedite matters by saying you don't care as long as it's not—well, just pick something, to show you're not completely indifferent.

Painters are always very busy and will do your whole house, inside and out, in ninety minutes using eight-foot-wide rollers unless you're careful. Insist on two coats over primer. Knots on Real Siding should be daubed with shellac; this will prevent their showing through for at least two weeks. If your house is covered with Fake Siding you don't need to paint it, as you probably know, because why else would anybody buy that stuff? Make sure the painter cleans all surfaces before beginning. Otherwise, candy wrappers and sluggish insects will end up permanently affixed to your dwelling.

Safe and Sound

A good security system is the first line of defense for your residential investment.

Security systems have always been with us. Old-fashioned models include moats, German shepherds and window ledges encrusted with broken glass and nails. Modern systems, though considerably more humane, make for a lot more stolen goods.

Today's state-of-the-art setup includes smoke and motion sensors at strategic locations around your home which, when activated, set off a pierc-

ing alarm that will cause your neighbors to do nothing just for spite. At the same time an automatic dialer calls fire and police departments, and three numbers of your choosing, with a prerecorded message and directions.

These systems are extremely delicate. Mine is activated by lightning as well as a toad that lives in the basement (see "Toad Note," p. 111). The smoke sensor goes ape whenever I make French toast. The cassette that's supposed to provide directions over the phone is impossible to understand, and the phone numbers the thing calls have to be updated regularly, ever since the estranged wife of a divorcing friend got a call announcing disaster at my house every time my toad went for a stroll.

Moats look better all the time.

When Enough Becomes Enough

The harmless wish to see what lies beneath the layers of paint and paneling can easily turn into an obsession to "bring the house back." *Newelpost Disease* is the insatiable compulsion to restore, regardless of whether or not it's worth the trouble.

Typically, a victim begins by wondering if the kitchen once had wainscoting. Mental deterioration follows rapidly. Woodstove literature starts arriving in the mail. Soon the master bedroom is papered with a tiny floral print. A spinning wheel appears in the living room. All the comfortable chairs disappear, replaced by the hard and rickety (but authentic) variety.

If you live with a victim of Newelpost Disease, you must be firm. Don't answer when asked if you think the triple-track storm windows are spoiling the façade. Refuse to discuss ornamental plasterwork, banister spindles or gabled pediments after nine P.M.

Contractor's Withdrawal

The contractor hates to finish a job almost as much as he hates to begin one. No matter how bad a deal he's made, how ugly he thinks the house is or what a son-of-a-bitch you are to work for, the contractor forms a bond with the site—that is, your house—that makes him insanely possessive. Treat your contractor gently when you notice he's shying away from the end of the job. Too abrupt an insistence that he leave, such as waving cash in his face and screaming, "Here! Take my money! Now get your things together and clear out!" could result in long-term psychological damage. Worse, he could walk off, and you'd have to find another contractor to finish up and listen to what he has to say about the work this contractor has just done.

The Visit of the Mother

When it's time for the weapon of last resort, tell the contractor your mother is coming. Even if your mother arrives to see the crew scampering over the lawn as she pulls into the drive, they'll be gone by the time she's in the doorway, where she'll

begin looking for dust. Your contractor is as scared of your mother as you are.

A Farewell to Beefy Arms

Eventually you pay for the last time. The crew moves on, leaving behind a little scrap wood, dozens of soda cans and a guide to investing on Wall Street. Be sure you hang on to your contractor's phone number and address, because it's an absolute certainty that there will be something wrong: a missing lock for the garage door, a lighting fixture that falls off.

Your contractor, if he's not in Barbados resting up for a month or two, will tell you "I'll be over as soon as I can." In the tradition of "Peace in Our Time," "I am not a crook" and "The check is in the mail," his words are not true.

Stop for a breather anyway. You're home at last.

Home Sweet Equity

Selling?

Time flies, particularly when mortgage payments are due. You're used to your house. You've put several local boys through college on what you pay them to rake your leaves. The tang of mold in the basement isn't so bad once you've lived with it awhile, and as long as everything's out of the north end by March nothing gets too soaked.

Ignoble House

You know you are fortunate. The fact that you're still able to arrange for the same repairs, year in, year out, means you've developed the kind of grit it takes to own a home. It also means your phones still work.

Yet who can blame the homeowner who looks around and asks: "Is that all there is?" There still isn't a decent Chinese restaurant within miles, and you've had it with patching the roof. Maybe you'd better start making some calls. Who knows how long it'll take to get a home improvement loan? As long as a roofer's waiting list?

One morning you'll wake up and want to sell. Not so fast.

Bridge Loan over Troubled Waters

You may need to sell one home in order to buy another. Your problem is simple: do you buy the home into which you need to move once you sell the one you're now in, or sell the home you're now in in order to get the money you need to buy the house you need to move into, once you sell the one you're now in?

Is a puzzlement.

No problem, say today's financial experts, who've solved the conundrum with the *bridge loan*, an arrangement that enables you to borrow against the equity in your home at interest rates that will make your eyeballs rotate in their sockets like ball bearings. Bridge loans are available

only from *mortgage brokers,* who are similar to bankers but dress more garishly. A bridge loan requires a formal closing just like the closing on your home except that you have to pay an extra set of lawyers and you don't even get a house out of it.

Primping

Before placing your home on the market, take a good look around and face the fact that it's in no condition to show to anyone.

Patrol your house with a little can of paint and dab at scuff marks. Straighten up the living room. Place vases of flowers all over the place.[1] When buyers come through, boil a vanilla bean. Play soft rock at subliminally low volume. Suddenly, it will hit you:

You're doing everything you thought was so ridiculous when you were looking.

Where Have All the Brokers Gone?

Remember what the brokers were like when you were looking to buy? How they'd call you up in the morning when it was still dark (and once during Thanksgiving dinner), just to bring word of a "peppy listing"? Remember how they explained

---

1. But be careful. You can go overboard with the flowers, causing buyers to think you're selling because of a death in the family. The vibe can be very off-putting.

that they were being at-
tentive to you *in particular* because they *liked*
you? After all, you don't
even pay for their time.
Remember all that?

Your broker's answering service.

How times change.

They're harder to reach now, and they're in
less of a hurry to get back to you. Eventually,
you'll have to deal with the broker's child. Now,
the children of real estate professionals are rigorously trained in telephone skills. Any broker's
kid strong enough to lift a receiver can take down
a name and number, give assurances that Mom
or Dad will get back to you, and hope you have a
nice day.

This courtesy is intended strictly for buyers.
Messages from people with houses for sale are
thrown out or forgotten altogether. The moral:
Never tell a broker's child you're trying to sell
your house.

Listing Your House

There are a variety of ways to work with realtors.
An *open listing* means you've crisscrossed the
area, dropping off keys with every brokerage for
miles around. An open listing is a sign of des-
peration and won't even get you into the Multi-
ple Listing Service, that grimy booklet of homes
on the market stacked up in vast numbers in su-
permarkets and banks, right by the wastepaper
basket.

There's also an *exclusive right to sell* or an *exclusive agency listing*. Which is best for you?

The Grim Truth

It won't matter much which option you choose.

It won't matter when you put it on the market, either, or how carefully you plot strategy with the sympathetic broker who thinks your sweet, little rundown place might be sold for a tidy sum— if you're not too greedy.

How you try to sell your house doesn't matter because putting your house up for sale has an extraordinary effect on the market. Once hot and strong, the market suddenly goes cool and soft. All the househunters saddle up and move on to the next town, perhaps because the local housing board requires prospective home buyers to test for drug use when they put down a binder, an innovative way to control the growth in your community by making it unlikely anyone will budge in or out. Selling your house is just too big a deal to think about right now, especially while the patio is the way it is. (How much would it cost to fix, you wonder.)

You're used to the place by now. Might as well stay, at least until you can afford to buy a place you'll really love, a real *home*.

Until then, what's the matter with where you are now?

Appendices

Appendix I: Hobby from Hell

The realest part of real property is land, and no part of your residence affords greater opportunity for expenditure, grief and backbreaking labor than gardening. It would take an entire book to sketch the full horror that is gardening. There's garbage to be sorted for compost, and equipment to be cleaned, and all that time poking around in dirt planting things and picking bugs off. There's storage, too. Where do you think the mower, rake, trowel, hoe, shears, knee pads and all those filthy clothes and terrible hats are going to end up? In your garage, of course, formerly the residence of your car.

The very thought of gardening tuckers me out.

A Note on Birdscape

Nothing makes for more hideous grounds décor than devices for attracting birds. Plexiglass feeders, stone birdbaths, hunks of suet hung from branches in winter, bread crumbs on the porch in summer—each is quite unattractive by itself. Taken together, they create a slovenly appearance that you can justify only in terms of the new species you've drawn to the area. Buy a birdwatcher's guide and keep track of the birds you see on your lawn. Some will build nests in your gutters; the nests will clog the downspouts, and water will back up right into your house (see "Water Problems," p. 72). In the morning, you'll be awakened by the *dawn chorus*, a sort of avian pep rally during which thousands of birds sing their characteristic melodies while doing their business on your car. Be sure you leave some slack in your budget for extra car washes.

Appendix II: Closing Interruptus

For no more than fifty dollars in singles (fresh bills are best), you can sabotage your closing at the last minute. Crunch up the bills individually until they're about the size of cocktail meatballs. Conceal them on your person or in a briefcase that you keep closed. Once you're sure you're willing to do anything to get out of the deal, gesture wildly and shout: "Look! It's raining money!" As everyone looks up, fling the singles into the air. Slip away in the feeding frenzy of lawyers, brokers and bankers that ensues. Only the seller will notice you leaving.

This is not a device to be employed casually, since it will mean you forfeit your deposit and invite several types of legal action. Many homeowners come to feel in later years, though, that the financial loss would have been worth it.

Appendix III: Mi Casa Es Su Casa

Welcoming others into your home is a necessary passage of home ownership. The threat of company is also the goad some homeowners need to remove the last traces of renovation (even though the workmen may have left years ago). Others don't feel they've really moved in until they've thrown a big party. Such people are not well, but even in ancient Greece a celebration in a new home was the traditional way to curry favor with the deities and get the contractors to finish.

A housewarming is also a polite way to ask for gifts.

Housewarming Tips

◆ Serve pale dips and salads. Stray plaster dust and wood chips blend right in. Don't cook anything that might set off the smoke alarm.

◆ Don't get angry at the guests when they track footprints on the carpet. Whose dust is it, anyway?

◆ Keep the house tour brief. Few of your guests want to see the boiler. Do not discuss the waste removal system unless specifically asked.

How to Be a Perfect Guest

The homeowner's relationship to the dwelling is riddled with morbid complexity. The house is boss, lover, pet, child, master, servant, creditor—it's disgusting, really. The homeowner will share this obsession with anyone who will listen. A perfect guest is one who shows more interest in the basement than in the view. Homeowners love to drone on about the guts of the house, like proud parents raving about their little one's poop.

Good Things to Say to Homeowners
"What an eye you have!"
"This is the original flooring, isn't it?"
"I see the finish work goes inside the closet. *Very good.*"
"It sits on the lot so nicely."
"What was here when you started?"[1]

Questions to Avoid
"Those branches block the view all year round?"
"How come *this* is in *this* room?"
"You suing anyone?"
"How far will you be from the nuke plant?"
"So what'd you pay?"[2]

---

1. Should your hosts begin to cry when you ask this question, change the subject.

2. Men are notably more upset by this question than women. Typically, a man would rather tell you his sperm count than what he paid for where he lives.

Note to homeowners: The wise homeowner will treat guests well. They can do much to make you feel better. A friend's enthusiastic appreciation of your home and what it's put you through will make him welcome at your place long after your calls and invitations have ceased to be returned.